W9-BWS-695

Cliques

Other Books in the Social Issues Firsthand Series:

SOCIAL ISSUES
FIRSTHAND

Cliques

Sharon R. Gunton, Book Editor

GREENHAVEN PRESS
A part of Gale, Cengage Learning

GALE
CENGAGE Learning™

Detroit • New York • San Francisco • New Haven, Conn • Waterville, Maine • London

Christine Nasso, *Publisher*
Elizabeth Des Chenes, *Managing Editor*

© 2010 Greenhaven Press, a part of Gale, Cengage Learning.

Gale and Greenhaven Press are registered trademarks used herein under license.

For more information, contact:
Greenhaven Press
27500 Drake Rd.
Farmington Hills, MI 48331-3535
Or you can visit our Internet site at gale.cengage.com

For product information and technology assistance, contact us at

Gale Customer Support, 1-800-877-4253

For permission to use material from this text or product, submit all requests online at www.cengage.com/permissions

Further permissions questions can be emailed to permissionrequest@cengage.com

Articles in Greenhaven Press anthologies are often edited for length to meet page requirements. In addition, original titles of these works are changed to clearly present the main thesis and to explicitly indicate the author's opinion. Every effort is made to ensure that Greenhaven Press accurately reflects the original intent of the authors. Every effort has been made to trace the owners of copyrighted material.

Cover photograph copyright Andresr, 2009. Used under license from Shutterstock.com.

LIBRARY OF CONGRESS CATALOGING-IN-PUBLICATION DATA

Cliques / Sharon R. Gunton, book editor.
    p. cm. -- (Social issues firsthand)
    Includes bibliographical references and index.
    ISBN 978-0-7377-4029-5 (hardcover)
    1. Teenagers--Psychology. 2. Cliques (Sociology) 3. Peer pressure in adolescence. 4. Interpersonal relations in children. 5. Interpersonal conflict in children. I. Gunton, Sharon
    HQ796.C595 2009
    305.235--dc22

                                                    2009018940

Printed in the United States of America
1 2 3 4 5 6 7 13 12 11 10 09

Contents

Chapter 1: Examining Clique Behavior

Chapter 2: Victims and Perpetrators

Chapter 3: Finding Personal Identity

Foreword

Social issues are often viewed in abstract terms. Pressing challenges such as poverty, homelessness, and addiction are viewed as problems to be defined and solved. Politicians, social scientists, and other experts engage in debates about the extent of the problems, their causes, and how best to remedy them. Often overlooked in these discussions is the human dimension of the issue. Behind every policy debate over poverty, homelessness, and substance abuse, for example, are real people struggling to make ends meet, to survive life on the streets, and to overcome addiction to drugs and alcohol. Their stories are ubiquitous and compelling. They are the stories of everyday people—perhaps your own family members or friends—and yet they rarely influence the debates taking place in state capitols, the national Congress, or the courts.

The disparity between the public debate and private experience of social issues is well illustrated by looking at the topic of poverty. Each year the U.S. Census Bureau establishes a poverty threshold. A household with an income below the threshold is defined as poor, while a household with an income above the threshold is considered able to live on a basic subsistence level. For example, in 2003 a family of two was considered poor if its income was less than $12,015; a family of four was defined as poor if its income was less than $18,810. Based on this system, the bureau estimates that 35.9 million Americans (12.5 percent of the population) lived below the poverty line in 2003, including 12.9 million children below the age of eighteen.

Commentators disagree about what these statistics mean. Social activists insist that the huge number of officially poor Americans translates into human suffering. Even many families that have incomes above the threshold, they maintain, are likely to be struggling to get by. Other commentators insist that the statistics exaggerate the problem of poverty in the United States. Compared to people in developing countries, they point out, most so-called poor families have a high quality of life. As stated by journalist Fidelis Iyebote, "Cars are owned by 70 percent of 'poor' households. . . . Color televisions belong to 97 percent of the 'poor' [and] videocassette recorders belong to nearly 75 percent. . . . Sixty-four percent have microwave ovens, half own a stereo system, and over a quarter possess an automatic dishwasher."

However, this debate over the poverty threshold and what it means is likely irrelevant to a person living in poverty. Simply put, poor people do not need the government to tell them whether they are poor. They can see it in the stack of bills they cannot pay. They are aware of it when they are forced to choose between paying rent or buying food for their children. They become painfully conscious of it when they lose their homes and are forced to live in their cars or on the streets. Indeed, the written stories of poor people define the meaning of poverty more vividly than a government bureaucracy could ever hope to. Narratives composed by the poor describe losing jobs due to injury or mental illness, depict horrific tales of childhood abuse and spousal violence, recount the loss of friends and family members. They evoke the slipping away of social supports and government assistance, the descent into substance abuse and addiction, the harsh realities of life on the streets. These are the perspectives on poverty that are too often omitted from discussions over the extent of the problem and how to solve it.

Greenhaven Press's *Social Issues Firsthand* series provides a forum for the often-overlooked human perspectives on society's most divisive topics of debate. Each volume focuses on one social issue and presents a collection of ten to sixteen narratives by those who have had personal involvement with the topic. Extra care has been taken to include a diverse range of perspectives. For example, in the volume on adoption, readers will find the stories of birth parents who have made an adoption plan, adoptive parents, and adoptees themselves. After exposure to these varied points of view, the reader will have a clearer understanding that adoption is an intense, emotional experience full of joyous highs and painful lows for all concerned.

The debate surrounding embryonic stem cell research illustrates the moral and ethical pressure that the public brings to bear on the scientific community. However, while nonexperts often criticize scientists for not considering the potential negative impact of their work, ironically the public's reaction against such discoveries can produce harmful results as well. For example, although the outcry against embryonic stem cell research in the United States has resulted in fewer embryos being destroyed, those with Parkinson's, such as actor Michael J. Fox, have argued that prohibiting the development of new stem cell lines ultimately will prevent a timely cure for the disease that is killing Fox and thousands of others.

Each book in the series contains several features that enhance its usefulness, including an in-depth introduction, an annotated table of contents, bibliographies for further research, a list of organizations to contact, and a thorough index. These elements—combined with the poignant voices of people touched by tragedy and triumph—make the Social Issues Firsthand series a valuable resource for research on today's topics of political discussion.

Introduction

When Colorado sociologists Patricia and Peter Adler did an eight-year study of young people in their community and wrote *Peer Power: Preadolescent Culture and Identity* in 1998, they identified and named four groups: roughly 35 percent of their subjects were in the Popular Clique. This group was attractive, charismatic, often affluent, and got attention from students and teachers. The Fringe accounted for about 10 percent of the preadolescents. They mimicked the popular set, sometimes even becoming temporary friends of the popular clique members. The Middle Friendship Circles were 45 percent of the research group. They formed small groups of several friends who shared a certain look and interest or lifestyle. They might be geeks, Goths, or other groups, and were labeled unpopular, but did not really want to play the popularity game. The Loners were the final 10 percent, and they had no close friends.

These various groups, their identities and their actions, have always fascinated young adults. Consequently, the interaction between different cliques has been the subject of movies and books for decades.

Films About Cliques

A classic example of a film that focused intently on this subject was John Hughes's *The Breakfast Club* (1985). The story involves five high school students: a jock named Andrew Clark, a nerd named Brian Johnson, a tough named John Bender, a princess named Claire Standish, and a misfit named Allison Reynolds. They are forced to stay in the library together for detention. During this time, they find that they have much in common and learn to like and respect each other. Hughes captures the early preconceptions they have about one another and their total unwillingness to acknowledge each other.

Rather than being stereotypes, the characters are revealed to have deep-felt fears, doubts, dreams, and hopes, and they grow and improve after getting to know one another. Hughes seems to say that if the clique labels can be ignored, surprising friendships and romances might develop.

Often, however, films have dealt instead with the manipulation and debasement practiced by members of popular cliques on others in their school or community. In these films, young adults are engaged in using their power amongst their peers to redirect others' lives, using them as pawns. Movies like *She's All That* (1999), *Clueless* (1995), and *Cruel Intentions* (1999) depict the beautiful people in domineering and conniving roles. The fact that all three films are based on much earlier written works (George Bernard Shaw's *Pygmalion* [1914], Jane Austen's *Emma* [1815], and Pierre Choderlos de Laclos's *Les Liaisons dangereuses* [1782], respectively) shows that the subject of domination and manipulation is timeless.

Two Popular Fictional Works on Cliques

Whenever cliques are mentioned, two popular works are often cited: the film *Mean Girls* (2004) and *The Clique* series of novels (published beginning in 2004). The former is a story based on the groundbreaking book on adolescent female aggression and cliques, Rosalind Wiseman's *Queen Bees and Wannabes* (2002). In the screenplay written by Tina Fey, a naïve and trusting sixteen-year-old named Cady Heron has just moved to Evanston, Illinois after twelve years of living (and being homeschooled) in Africa. She enters the high school social scene as a blank slate and learns all about female behavior in her school. Because of her crush on a boy in her math class, she allows herself to be influenced by Regina George, the popular girl who used to be his girlfriend. Little by little, Cady becomes as mean as the girls she once disdained. Revealing the dilemma faced by many of the others in her school, Cady is perplexed by the fact that: "I hated Regina, but I wanted her to like me." Eventually, Cady learns to trust her own judgment and make true friends.

In the bestselling *Clique* novels, written by Lisi Harrison, the main characters are Claire Lyons (newly transplanted from Florida to Westchester County in New York) and Massie Block (the wealthy and spoiled leader of the popular group at their school). In the first novel, Claire shows up for her first day of school in unsophisticated clothes and becomes the object of ridicule. She is teased and ostracized until she devises a scheme to get back at Massie, but after she is found out, she realizes that she wants to be true to who she is and actually ends up helping Massie. The series further develops their characters, as well as introducing other characters. Sales of the books have been brisk and libraries have waiting lists for their copies. A film has been made from the first novel (*The Clique* [2008]).

A Real-Life Depiction

In the documentary *American Teen* (2008) by Nanette Burstein, several real-life high school seniors explain their behavior and define their understanding of social status and cliques. Each of the four teens who are the main focus of the film are typical representatives of the main cliques found in high schools: Megan Krizmanich is popular (she is even called a Queen Bee by one of the other students), Colin Clemens is a jock (the star of the basketball team), Jake Tusing calls himself a band geek and often feels as if he doesn't fit in with the other students, and Hannah Bailey is creative and unconventional and feels that no one in the conservative school understands her. From affluent, popular Megan to shy, sensitive Jake, all of the teens go through their last year of high school trying to decide what they want to do with their futures, how to handle their relationships, and how to find some sort of acceptance and contentment. An example of the impermeability of the groups occurs when a jock named Mitch starts to date artistic Hannah. He initially says it shouldn't matter that they are from different groups and he loves her personality and quirkiness, but after she comes to a party with his friends and there is palpable awkwardness, he breaks up with her. Burstein underscores the fact that each of the students has become identified with a certain group and they function within what they themselves call "the caste system" at their school. And, unlike the fictional depictions mentioned above, the teens do not learn to break down the barriers. Their roles stay the same; in some cases, there is little change even after graduation.

Audience Appeal

Critics are divided about the value of depicting clique behavior in books, television shows, and movies. Some feel that showing bullies who are popular encourages young adults to adopt that behavior, even if the script or book text seems to denounce it as odious. But some critics feel that the formation of cliques is actually quite normal and eases the transition of teens from family into the wider world. While they do not condone the behavior of some clique members, they recognize that teens who are navigating the social maze at their schools are fascinated by pop culture depictions (especially accurate depictions) of what is happening to them and their friends.

Social Issues Firsthand: Cliques presents personal narratives about the issue from a number of perspectives, focusing on the behavior of cliques, those who are acting as perpetrators and those who are victimized, and how finding personal identity helps young people counteract the influence of the group. The following viewpoints demonstrate the sensitive nature of the issue and provide a foundation for further discussion.

SOCIAL ISSUES
FIRSTHAND

CHAPTER 1

Examining
Clique Behavior

Bullying Girls In and Out of Cliques

Chelsea Caplan

In this selection, high school student Chelsea Caplan describes two prominent factors in the lives of teenage girls: the importance of appearance and the way they treat each other. She points out that members of cliques tend to dismiss those outside their groups and even mistreat those in their groups. She proposes a simple and straightforward solution to spare girls' feelings, their confidence, and perhaps even their lives.

When the movie *Mean Girls* came out a few years ago, every girl seemed to fall in love with it. Why? Because every single one of us can relate to a group of girls who put themselves above everyone else; who are dismissive, rude and harsh to outsiders of their clique, and are even fake and backstabbing even when it's a girl within their own group.

All these things may sound like they belong in a movie, but as we all know all this is sadly true in real life. It happens every day, starting way back in elementary school.

I once baby-sat for a 3rd grader who, even at her age of eight years old, felt the competition to look good and wear brand names like Abercrombie [and Fitch] because her girlfriends liked to wear Abercrombie together.

This may seem like a problem that would only occur for kids in elementary school, but we all know that the problem of wearing, saying and doing the right thing is an issue that girls have to deal with from elementary school all the way up to high school, and maybe even college.

Chelsea Caplan, "Chicks in Cliques: Bullying Girls in Schools," *Hartford Informer*, April 10, 2008, pp. 1–2. Copyright © 2008 Informer. Reproduced by permission.

People wonder why some kids lack so much self-confidence, but if you look at the relationships that a lot of kids form at a very early age, we have all been betrayed, excluded and laughed at.

In 8th grade, my best friend set me up with a guy and then afterwards decided that she liked him and tried to have him go out with her, even though she knew that we were dating.

Another friend got jealous when I joined a youth group, which took up a lot of my time, so she told my youth group that I was failing school, which would have limited my activities in the group. Fortunately, that only worked until my name was printed in our local *Gazette* under the honor students list.

That was payback enough. But this is nothing compared to what I have seen in my own high school and with my own friends. I am sure everyone has a story about some of [the] mean things that they have seen girls do from high school and middle school.

We All Need to Change

Why do girls feel the need to belittle and undermine each other? We each crave a close bond and friendship with one another, yet we also manipulate, criticize and hurt each other, all for no explainable reason.

And these seemingly petty, stupid and immature actions don't seem like anything too important, but just looking at suicide rates and the reasons behind most of them, you will see a lot of these victims were teased, isolated and excluded from social settings.

Even if girls survive the cattiness of adolescent girls, internal scars can be remain and leave adult women insecure and lacking self-confidence all because of some middle school kids' cruel intentions 20, 30 or maybe even 40 years ago.

None of us wants to be put out or let down, so why do we do it to others? Why can't we just leave others we don't get along with alone?

If we don't get along, instead of feeling the need to bring each other down just because we have that power, why don't girls just try not associating with the people they don't like?

After all, isn't that a lot easier in the first place? It takes less energy, compared to always thinking of a way to hurt the other person, not to mention you are being a mature adult by doing so.

I know the cattiness of female adolescence will probably never come to an end, but if girls just tried to be a little nicer to one another at least it wouldn't be so bad.

What It Means to Belong

Anne Fleming

Anne Fleming is an author and teacher of creative writing. In this selection she describes her social experiences from age 12 to age 18. She gives an account of the various groups she belonged to, how they interacted, and how they shared their enthusiasms. Her essay portrays cliques in a favorable light, showing that when members are loyal and supportive in their dealings with each other and tolerant of others, a group can be a source of true camaraderie and bring the comfort of companionship and acceptance.

In the dining room, filling out the forms that will match me up with a kid from Quebec for my pending *visite interprovinciale*, my mother and I have a big fight. You have to put a tick next to "outgoing" or "reserved." Mom insists I am reserved. I say I'm outgoing. In fact, both are true. I'm socially outgoing and emotionally reserved, though I don't have the wherewithal at age twelve to make that distinction. Mom wins the fight, as she usually does. I end up with a painfully shy and awkward girl with whom I have nothing in common. Describing her later to friends, I slap a thumb-and-forefinger L to my forehead and say "Loser!" But that's not the point here.

The point here is about being socially outgoing but emotionally reserved. This means a number of things for my friendships: 1) They tend to be less about the exchange of intimacies than the exchange of jokes; 2) They start in the public sphere—in class, in the halls, at band rehearsal, in the showers after swim practice, on the way to track meets, on ski team road trips—and stay there unless the other person initiates. Calling people up and asking them to do things makes me feel like a porcupine with its belly exposed. Bad enough to reveal you like someone, but to reveal you presume they might like you, too? Aaaaaah. Too vulnerable, too vulnerable; 3) I am good in a group.

I love groups. Yeah, they can be exclusionary and danger-ous, cliquey and inwardly conformist and yada yada, but even so they can be fabulous. And then there are the moments of true groupness, those rare but exquisite times when it feels ev-eryone is equal and respected and liked, when it's clear you're all wonderful, inventive, funny people and that you're in this together, whatever *this* is. Your hearts expand, sproing-sproing-sproing like the Grinch's, and what you feel is love for the whole world, for the variety and splendor of humanity.

Then There Was Thirteen

On the way to the subway that'll take us to indoor track prac-tice, we jostle and smoke and talk about quitting, though none of us is really addicted. Andrew's already quit. Lorelei's going to. "Yeah, me too," says Chris, lighting up.

We roll our student transit tickets in our fingers till they're soft and pliable, then peel them apart to drop one-half in the fare box, print side up. Ariel goes further and does it with a child's ticket. She's five-nine and has to start doing a sort of bent-knee duckwalk at the edge of the fare booth to pass for under twelve. We snigger on one side of the turnstile and guf-faw on the other.

We biff the punch-button on the transfer box with our fists, snag our unneeded transfers and fold them in half, then slip them between our first and second fingers, fold the sides down left and right, and blow into the slit, making a high-pitched whine that out-decibels the blade-of-grass-between-the-fingers trick by an impressive factor. Decent.

We don't even dare each other anymore, just do it if we feel like it: stand on the yellow warning strip lining the platform's, edge, confident and adrenalized, all in a row.

Subway's not going to hit ya, but it sure feels like it the first time, feels like it's going to take your nose off. By now it's kind of a mystical thing, planting feet on yellow, hearing the thunder and squeal of the approaching train, feeling the warm musty breath of the tunnels washing over you like dragon wind as the hurtling silver train pistons air ahead of it, whoosh, into the station. Then the harder bam of air from the train front hits and the racing metal's suddenly a handsbreadth from your face, and there you all are, cool and daring, loose-kneed and easy.

We saunter onto the train, take up a lot of seats, put our feet up, swing from the hang rails, fake each other out with kung fu kicks checked at the last second. Ditto with eye pokes and face slaps. When it comes to tripping, though, there's no pretending. It's real, it's constant. Right then it's the entire point of our existence.

We make sidelong agreements to car-hop next stop without telling this week's target. Act casual coming into the stop, snake into action, leave whoever it is gaping in their seat or tearing after us trying to join us in the next car before the doors close. Maybe the kid manages to stab a hand through the converging rubber of the doors and yank them apart or maybe the rubber sandwiches a torso or a leg, doesn't matter, we're killing ourselves. Even better is leaving the kid on the platform, the look on that face. Next stop we all get out and wait. Unless the kid's a real idiot, then forget it. Decent, man. We're effin' great. We don't even know how young we are.

At the exhibition grounds, at the grand, old-smelling, warehouse-like track where the feet of national-level university athletes make the raised red-rubber-covered wooden running oval thunder, we stretch and train, inspired, ambitious, and no longer rambunctious. We're good. We're the best in the city. Not me personally, but we, we are, that's why we own the tube from north to south that gets us here. We're the best. We're obnoxious. Decent.

What Happened at Fourteen

We're on the bus. Bus 301, one of three taking our high school band to New York. Actually, to be precise, Syosset, Long Island. Bus 301, the Bingo Bus, because Nick and I, rummaging around in the cabinet above the back seat, have discovered a raft of orange bingo cards with little black slide-over windows, the detritus of biddies before us. Naturally, we pass 'em out and play.

Put me on a bus, I'm going to go to the back. The back's better. Just is. Back of whatever: class, assembly, airplane. Sure, the bus's hindquarters are bouncier, more nausea-inducing, closer to the urine-tinged blue chemical smell of the toilet, but that's the price you pay to be loud and awake and maybe doing an illicit thing or two.

I'm sitting next to Jason, don't know how that happened, but there you go. Jason is lead clarinetist, concert master, actor, cartoonist, publisher of a lampoon called "The Poor Nam's Almanac." Blue eyes, dark lashes, slightly pockmarked skin, tired of high school, beyond it, itching to leave it behind. Only a few weeks to go and he will.

Saucy, vivacious Chewie, flute, is draped over the seat ahead of us, while Nick (tall, droopy, black-clad), also flute, curls over from behind, and nicotine-stained-fingered French horn Sue leans across the aisle. Bingo lasted us longer than you'd think possible—an hour, maybe even two. Now we're working on "Silly Notes," a parody of the music department's cute-ish and earnest "Musical Notes."

"Silly Notes" is how it sounds. It has all the trappings of a newsletter—Volume I, Issue 1, date, masthead—plus Jason's cartoon of the Bingo Bus with Bingo cards a-flyin' out the back next to clouds of smoke billowing from the bathroom window. It's filled with made-up gossip ("Contrary to popular opinion, Rebecca 'Chewie' Carver does not eat nails for breakfast. She eats them for lunch"), stupid advice columns ("Ask Ene," Ene Lomp being the new music teacher, whom we suspect was hired for her blondeness, makeup, and three-inch heels), and inane activities ("Activity #19: Hold this up to the window and read it backwards"). Best of all, somehow, "Silly Notes" is written on paper towel from the bathroom, soft, hearty blonde rag stock with a ready built-in fold. It's perfect.

We don't know it yet, but we're approaching groupness here. We don't know it because we're still testing each other, still feeling each other out in this new proximity, different from our usual band-room rootedness: trombones back, trumpets across the way, clarinets front right, flutes front left, double reeds pinched in the middle, and so on. This is just the bus ride: whatever's going to happen is going to happen in New York, right? The stories we're living now are warm-ups to the stories we'll live when we get there. This is interim. This is filling time.

When the Group Leaves Its Familiar Setting

We drive through the city to get to Long Island, faces plastered at the window in wonder, and pull up in the late evening at a suburban high school. Off the bus, our little coterie splits up into the grade-based associations that had dissolved on it. Also into billeting groups of two and three.

So here we are.

New York.

Okay, Syosset.

And?

Nothing. Syosset is completely forgettable, New York slightly less so. Five days, a couple of band concerts, a "social," a UN trip, a final afternoon where we get dumped in some not-so-good part of the city and told to reconvene in a couple of hours. Within half a block we get hit up by eight drug dealers peddling substances I don't even know what they are.

I don't think it's just me, either, because *whomp*, the cohesion when we're back on the bus is immediate, like *this* is the real world, *this* is the real holiday, here on the Bingo Bus, another twelve hours home stretching ahead of us, another edition of "Silly Notes" already in production. This one sports a cartoon of a battered and vandal-stripped Bus 301 and the caption "The Bingo Bus 15 minutes after being parked at 47th and 71st"—or whatever the streets actually were.

It's a moment of pure groupness. Amazingly, it lasts the whole ride.

Released from the established strictures of "who our friends are" by the captivity of the bus, we are Us and we are the Bingo Bus. At the back the us-ness feels as dense and certain as an India-rubber ball. Our bond will endure beyond the bus, beyond the school year, into the summer and the following year, when Jason is at university and we bury the post in an avalanche of letters full of fondness and wit, for aren't the group of us the cleverest and funniest of the band, aren't we naturally meant to bend our heads together like this to skewer banality and pomposity? Isn't the air full of love and admiration, of our waking breath mixed with the breath of the rest of the sleeping bus? When we trundle into the school parking lot and roll off the bus, don't we know this parting is different from the last one, aren't we mercury from a broken thermometer, careening off in little beads but longing to merge, to glop back together in an inky pool? Don't we say things like "I thought the bus was gonna be a drag, but it turned out to be the best part of the trip" (Nick), and "How am I going to live without the Bingo Bus?" (Chewie), and "Well, coeditor?" (Jason) "Well?" (Me). "See ya around."

But as it turns out, we don't see each other around. I hear from a third party Jason has found out, to his shock, that I'm only in grade nine. He'd thought grade eleven at least. I sense the doom in that revelation, but unwilling to believe the India rubber of the Bingo Bus has transmogrified to sponge—rotting sponge—I go against my usual retiring practices and, yearbook in hand, attempt to track Jason down. He's elusive. Deliberately? Chances are.

He's so elusive that, on the very last day of classes, I grab the same third party to take my yearbook to drama class with her for Jason to sign. I nervously await the outcome. What will he write? Something funny, no doubt, some hilarious reference to our many in-jokes, our fine, enduring camaraderie, our essential belongingness via our matching worldviews and senses of humor.

I get the yearbook back, thank her coolly, and wait for a time I can read it in private. Check the front. Nothing. The back. Nope. Skim the middle. Stop. My heart crawls. There's a large picture of him in the school play and across it he has signed his name, just his name, first and last, as if I were a fan and he a celebrity. Betrayal, this is betrayal. But instead of berating him, I berate myself. Stupid, stupid, stupid. Exposed belly, ripped-out guts, shame.

My Friends at Fifteen

On a sunny evening in June, five of us meet in a park around the corner from the subway stop by the Roxy Theatre. Last fall, Suzan and I sold homemade *Rocky Horror Picture Show* kits to Roxy patrons. Now the theatre's showing *Eraserhead*. Suzan's seen it, loved it, orchestrated this outing. I only know it's supposed to be weird. This is good. Suzan and I are into weird.

Suzan is skinny and neurotic and en route to being a full-on punker. The "z" is new—last year she was Susan—but it fits, she makes a good Suzan. I am goofier; my weirdness involves wearing a blue-and-white striped toque throughout the day, quoting too much Monty Python, and—the part of it I can't help and don't want to anyway—emitting a murky kind of butchness. Suzan and I are pals. We range all over the city exploring new neighborhoods. In boring classes we take turns writing a story called "The Continuing Adventures of Ralph and Spot and Him." We write silly poems and sign them "SIN-

POT Productions." (Suzan wants to be a filmmaker and has to have a production company.) SINPOT stands for School Is Not Penguins Or Toenails.

The others with us are Sue, Lisa, and Stephanie, a trio of femmy smart girls from band. Occasionally, when they invite me—and since they're friendly and nice, they often do—I become an adjunct of their group. So the *we* of this evening combines two we's I'm a part of.

In the park, we prepare for the weirdness of *Eraserhead* by passing a wineskin full of red plonk. I don't drink, don't like the taste of red wine. I smoke cigarillos instead. But we're all in high spirits. Groupness is in the air.

Wine consumed, winetips savored, we waltz down the street to the theatre, take our seats, and watch the credits roll over what looks like sperm in outer space. Next there's a shock-headed big-cheeked fella in a trench coat staring dumbly up at his puny rooms. Then the rooms themselves, in which there's a clanky rad [radiator] and a baby resembling a turkey. That's as far as we get, when from beside me comes a gurgling noise and a smell—red wine vomit. Gak. She's not leaning her head forward and barfing on the floor, she's letting it burble out and down the front of her white shirt. Lisa. Jesus. She's scaring me. What kind of shape is she in not to even lean forward?

I wait for somebody else to notice and take action, but no, the burbling continues. I should say something, a simple "Are you all right?" but I can't, I'm dumb. Instead I alert the person on the other side of her. "Hey," I wheeze. "Suzan."

And suddenly there is action, there are hands on her back, there are murmured queries, there's the whole group of us up and leading her out of the theatre and to the bathroom, where everyone but me crowds around, solicitous. I don't have the stomach for it, nor do I know what's required. The others do, apparently. They seem to thrive on this, on being needed, on the kick of emergency mode, on their own selflessness.

They buzz with arrangements. Who will take her home? Where are her parents? Out of the house? Good, we can call her brother to come pick her up. They are effective, efficient, caring. They are good friends, they are girlfriends, they know how to be girlfriends, they're a group. They're experiencing a moment of pure groupness and I'm not in it. I'm not quite a girl.

Student Council at Sixteen

In grade eleven, I eat my lunch in the student council office. The cast of characters in the student council office is this: 1) Ameen, president, a skinny guy who dresses like a forty-year-old in neatly pressed shirts and dress pants and has a host of odd obsessions, including the TV show *Caged Women*, which he calls *Caged Wimmings*. "In a pig's eye," says Ameen. "Deadly." "Deb-outs." "Never-the-nonetheless." He has a wonderful velvet voice with a Kenya-British accent. Ameen misses Nairobi, so he cranks the heat in the student council office to 90°; 2) Heather, secretary, a hunchbacked gift who wears a leg brace and walks with crutches. Apart from Ameen, she gave the best-prepared speech of anyone on the election slate. She's smart, a little whiny, and suspicious. She likes to play by the rules and have things her way, which means she and Ameen butt heads on a regular basis; 3) Erin, social coordinator, who pops in once in a while to drop off or pick up stacks of papers; 4) Sarge, hanger-on, former water boy for the football team now grown into himself, a player of *Dungeons and Dragons*, a rock climber and outdoors-person. He teaches me to play *Go*, but I never quite catch on; 5) Diane, another hanger-on, a sexy, smart girl against whom I pit myself at paddleball. We debate the legitimacy of her favored stance—paddle facing away from the body and ball smacked out and downwards—versus mine, the more traditional (and difficult) upward bounce; 6) Me, hanger-on *numéro trois*, eater of butter tarts and Bugles (both filed under B in the filing cabinet), paddle-ball champion, ear to Heather and Ameen's tales about each other.

We are an odd bunch, something I really see only in retrospect. Or maybe I knew it then and liked it, as I liked the weirdness with Suzan. This is not a group for me in the same way other groups are groups. There's no cohesive *we* I take pride in. Perhaps that in itself is something to be proud of. What all of us do know is that we have a home in the student council office. We are not cafeteria drek, we are not the seething masses. We are—not overtly, not consciously, except maybe for Diane—the freaks. Not losers. Freaks. It's different. We all have friends outside the student council office, we all have larger social circles—we are well-liked, unostracized freaks. And yet here we gather, day after day, Ameen turning up the heat, Heather griping about the heat, Diane lounging on the couch, Sarge sitting on the counter contemplating his next move in *Go*, me hitting a little rubber ball attached with an elastic to a wooden paddle. There is comfort in this.

At the end of the year, Ameen invites me to the formal. I panic, thinking the unthinkable: *What will people think?* (Also: *Oh no, nip this in the bud now, you don't want more awkwardness later.*)

I say no. Ameen asks Diane. She says yes. Only then do I glimpse what kind of a date it is, an Ameen-as-president-needs-a-date date, not an Ameen-wants-to-date-Anne date. Only then do I know how I have betrayed him. How I have betrayed us.

Seventeen at Summer Camp

Nine of us. Staff, Camp Tapawingo. We're ringed on ratty sofas around the big room of the whitewashed 1930s cottage that serves as the staff lounge, looking at the floor or picking at our shoes. We're getting chewed out by Liz, the camp director.

29

Somehow she's found out a group of us collectively smoked a joint the night before, and this morning, somber and fierce, she called a staff meeting to say she wanted everyone involved to be at White Cottage at rest hour. All morning, between teaching our lessons and getting our campers to lunch, we've been conferring in anxious little pods. *Are you going? Are you? If we all go, what's she going to do? She can't fire a third of her staff. Who do you think she overheard?*

So here we are, nine of us. There'd be two more, but they paddled off this morning on a canoe trip with their campers. We have each smoked one-eleventh of a joint.

I want to protest, to say, "Look, it was nothing, I had two puffs, it was almost literally nothing," but I can't. We are in this together, and even if it's really Annabelle's fault (her drugs, her idea), we've gotta stand by her. Liz is wrong to take this so seriously. We're not a bunch of idiot stoners who're going to do this all the time and leave the campers to burn down their cabins. But there's no telling her that.

She says she's going to phone our parents. She's disappointed in us. How stupid could we be? She doesn't mind getting a whole new staff next year if it means she'll get people who are responsible, who care for the campers' safety. She goes on and on.

I like Liz. I respect her. I'd like to consider her a friend. So despite my inner protestations, I feel terrible. And, as she says, stupid. All this for two puffs of something that gives me less of a buzz than cigarillos. Yet, for this half hour—indeed, for the rest of the camp session, since Liz does not fire us, though she does call our parents—we're doubly a group. United in our sheepishness, distress, and chagrin, we also feel the charge like a current between us, that it's we nine here and not anyone else. As soon as we walk out of White Cottage, we've got us a name: The Nasty Nine. "Plus two!" someone adds, remembering the pair out on the trip, who confessed to Liz before leaving.

That's us. The Nasty Nine. $N^2 + 2$.

Looking Back at Eighteen

We wait out the remaining June of high school in backyards, drinking beer, listening to music. There are no wild parties. It's as if we're past that, or in some lull before we go on to wilder ones.

Sometimes the Goobs are there, sometimes not. The Goobs got their name from our leonine history teacher, Allan, presumably because he found them loud and slobbery. They're five guys ironic about everything, including their own goofball comedy. Their silent film about the Russian Revolution has a title card that reads "Serf's up!" after a shot of a hanged peasant. They run an election campaign parodying the base appeals of election campaigns. "Vote for Simon," runs their slogan, "he's no homo." They win.

These evenings, the Goobs suck back the cool ones and make fun of whatever takes their fancy. People who say "suck back the cool ones," for example. "Party hardy, man." "No, man, it's party *hearty*. Hearty. Like, Ho-ho-ho hearty. Where you been, man?" "No way, man, it's hard-y, like you're gonna party hard and you're just putting a -ee on the end." They go on like this for hours, until they find another party to go to. They're a group unto themselves, but they're also part of our group.

Mostly, though, it's Sue, Lisa, Stephanie, Emilia, John, Paul, and me.

Sue, Lisa, Stephanie, and Emilia are easy to be with, good conversationalists, funny. I think of them as "the Girls," even though I am a girl too. When John gives me his novel to read because he wants a female perspective, I think he should've given it to them. The Girls are in the novel, however, so giving it to them wasn't an option.

Paul and Sue are a couple now. Once, a few years ago, Paul and I exchanged a dry kiss in his bedroom instantly followed by . . . nothing. It was a nothing that negated the kiss, as if we'd agreed in that instant we were such good friends we'd had to try and now that we had and discovered there was zero to it, we could go on as ever.

This June is kind of the same. Nothing memorable happens, and yet this twilight we exist in is a perfect thing: the smell of cut grass and dying lilacs and John's American cigarettes, the strings of his guitar, the Goobs' rapid-fire banter, the balmy night breezes, the summer plans and exchanges of addresses, the five years of knowing each other dwelling in us. We all know exactly how Stephanie throws her head back when she laughs, how Emilia tilts her head forward. We know how Sue tucks her hair behind her ear and Lisa tosses hers behind her, we know the way Paul bounces when he walks and the way I lumber side to side, we know how John pushes up his glasses with his middle finger.

Though I'm ready to leave these people, ready for us to disperse, all my life I will look again for what we have here, and I will find it and lose it and find it and lose it over and over again.

Girls Shouldn't Tear Each Other Down

Ashley M.

In this article from Teen Ink Raw *web magazine, a connection is made between the desire for popularity and clique behavior. Teenager Ashley M. maintains that American culture promotes the importance of a preordained image, which causes attractive girls to become the leaders of groups and encourages mean acts to exclude or demean those who do not fit the image. She explains how this desire for popularity puts the focus on appearance, leading girls to put thinness before health.*

A tall, thin girl dressed in the latest fashion, her face covered with makeup, walks down the hall. This girl has a group of friends who all seem to have the right style, know all the right things to say, and everyone wants to be like them. This girl is known as the (typical) popular girl. For centuries people have wanted to be this kind of person. Admired, looked at, even envied. Unfortunately the behind-the-scenes reality is not as pretty. Hate and loathing [are] primary emotions that drives popularity to become . . . hurtful and damaging. . . .

Friendships Suffer for the Sake of Popularity

During my fifth-grade year I became friends with a girl in my class named Anna. The next school year came and we all graduated from being the all powerful fifth graders to being the small insignificant sixth graders. During this transition phase everyone started to change. Bodies developed and a need for popularity started to grow. With a new need to fit in, people started hurting others to gain status. I experienced a full-blown example of this cruelty. Half way into my sixth-grade year, Anna and I were eating lunch on a school bench when she turned and looked at me with a stubborn look on her face. I asked her what was wrong and she told me that she no longer wanted to be my friend; instead she wanted to hang out with the popular girls. I was shocked and hurt. With tears welling up within my eyes, I wondered how this had happened to me. Within the day I found myself a social outcast. Regrettably, I am not the only girl to have been hurt by the social ladder of the teen years.

Usually beginning around the time girls reach middle school social groups start to form. Days of being friends with someone because they shared their cookies with you start to end and the hurtful cycle of being popular starts to take effect. Because they want a place to belong, girls start forming these groups called cliques. If you look up the definition of "cliques" on Google it will tell you that it is an informal and restrictive social form of ruling. Rosalind Wiseman, author of *Queen Bees and Wannabes*, says there are seven levels of the clique scale. The top and head girl is called the Queen Bee. She is the ruling girl who—because of money, looks, charisma and other desirable traits—can be looked to as the leader. The second in command is called the "sidekick." This is the girl who wants to be just like the Queen Bee. She wants to look like the Queen, talk like the Queen, and be just as popular as the Queen. Then there is the "floater," this girl is friends with a lot of different groups and belongs to each one. There is another girl, the "torn bystander" who, although she knows better and might want to do the right thing, will do things that aren't right because she feels that her allegiance to her friends is more important. The "pleaser/wannabe/messenger" is just that, she will do anything to get on the Queen's good side. The "banker" is the girl with all the latest gossip; her role is to tell the group every story, true or untrue. Finally there is the "target." This is the girl who is the victim of the clique's wrath.

This last role that I have described is not just for a single girl, and being in a clique will not exempt any girl from feeling the wrath of jealousy or ignorance from other girls. Putting others down is how a lot of girls feel better about themselves. When talking about cliques, Amy Goldman Koss, author of *The Girls*, said "My theory is that all the other animals can poke each other with their horns when jockeying for position, but this is what girls do and have always done to get their position in the social scheme."

Media Images Promote Intolerance

Unfortunately girls do not just put others down. They put themselves down too. Last year as I was talking to my best friend the subject of our bodies came up. She said she felt that her bust wasn't "big enough." I recently talked to her over the summer and during the time since last year, she has developed; now she says she feels "too big." There will always be something for people to find wrong about themselves. In a study published in the *New York Times*, 3,700 breast implants were performed on teen girls in the year 2003. Studies showed that about 3,300 teen girls had overly-developed breasts reduced. According to the Nemours foundation, 333,000 people age 18 years and younger got plastic surgery in 2005. The most common procedures are otoplasty (pinning back ears), dermabrasion (to help hide acne scars), and breast reduction. This means that more and more girls are becoming "fake" in order to fit into the clone-like groups of popularity, instead of finding individual beauty to fit in.

The media is in no way helping this problem. In fact, the media is adding gas to the fire. Pictures of unhealthy, skinny models and articles that talk about losing weight portray an image to girls that tell them they aren't good enough. "Adolescent girls who frequently read dieting articles in magazines are more likely to engage in unhealthy weight control. . . ." A study on this theory was done by Patricia Van Den Berg, Ph.D., of the University of Minnesota in Minneapolis and was found to be true. Although the effect was more prominent with less socially accepted girls or in girls who already disliked their bodies, the girls studied showed signs of dieting, bulimia, and disliking their physical appearance. Every day on the television, posters, Internet, and other places, pictures of stick thin women with "perfect" bodies are shown. The truth is that the average U.S. American model is 5 foot 10 inches weighing 107 lbs, while the average North American woman is 5 foot 4 inches weighing 143 lbs. These models are not realistic. The wrong message is being sent to girls starting at a young age. The popular dolls today, known as Bratz, are a perfect example of this. Curvy girls in too much makeup and too little clothing are sending young girls the message that all girls need to look like little Angelina Jolie clones.

In order to get the super-small bodies that are so craved, girls will go to extreme methods. Anorexia is one of the popular and dangerous illnesses. Unfortunately along with the illness comes attention and sometimes popularity. In *USA Today* there was a story of a girl who asked how much weight had to be lost to be anorexic. This shows her concern was not with her health but with her popularity. Popularity is physically harming too many teen girls. As they try to fit in and change themselves teen girls conform to unhealthy eating habits.

The tall thin girl who seems to have it all really doesn't. Her friends are really enemies all fighting for her position by tearing each other down. When she looks in a mirror she hates what she sees. Never happy with her physical appearance she will go through anything in order to look just like the twig-like models on television. This girl is looked at by many to be almost "perfect," but in truth she is far from it. I've experienced a lot when it comes to teen girls, and I have learned that popularity isn't everything. What matters is having friends who like you for who you are and are willing to support you as well as help you like yourself.

When Cliques Can Coexist

Ned Vizzini

Author Ned Vizzini calls his book Teen Angst? Naaah. . . *"a quasi-autobiography" about his high school years. Before attending Hunter College, he was a student at Stuyvesant High School in New York City. In the following excerpt, Vizzini describes the high school's intense academic focus, which resulted in distinct cliques that could peacefully coexist.*

When I arrived at Stuyvesant High School on September 9, I was already terrified. I was terrified of high school girls; I was terrified of high school cliques; I was terrified because I'd been told that if you stood near Stuyvesant at 8:00 A.M., the wave of teenagers going to class would trample you. You'd be ground into the ground. I'd heard that some people died that way.

Turned out I didn't need to be so terrified. True, I didn't do too well with those high school girls. And the cliques got on my nerves. But the wave of teenagers going to class became my friends, and I became one of them: head lowered, hood raised, sleepwalking into school with my heavy backpack, like everybody else.

Stuyvesant High School has been called "the crown jewel of the New York City public school system" and "the best high school in America." It's a big, beige, brick place: 3,000 kids, ten stories high, with its own *bridge*. New York politicians decided they didn't need students getting run over on their way to the crown jewel, so they built a bridge over a highway to ensure us safe access. And that's just for starters.

Stuy has a marble lobby with chandeliers straight out of the Plaza Hotel and the school's motto carved in stone: *Pro scienta atque sapienta* [For Science and Wisdom]. There are three elevators and seven escalators, the computer rooms have new computers, the halls are fresh and clean, and even the bathrooms sparkle. It's like going to school at Club Med. My dad has a theory that the whole place was financed by the Mafia as a scheme to jack up surrounding property values. It cost one hundred twenty million bucks to build.

The Stuy-High Student Body

I came to school that first day with a sci-fi paperback tucked under my arm. I wasn't the only one. Stuy was full of kids with books; every other person seemed to have one, to defend against social interaction. I saw people going to school reading books, and walking through the halls with their faces buried in books. As the year progressed, the paperbacks gave way to fat textbooks, but the result was the same—everybody had a book.

Besides that, the only common thread among Stuy students was that we'd all passed "The Stuy Test." Admission to the school was based solely on a special test called the SSH-SAT, given in eighth grade. The test was supposed to keep Stuy chockfull of smart, industrious kids, but somehow that didn't work with my class. We were a random collection of nerds, jocks, geniuses, potheads, drunks, tortured poets, young Republicans, shifty-eyed loners, and just plain idiots. That first day, I met a freshman who was taking calculus and a twenty-two-year-old who still hadn't graduated. I saw girls who looked like they spent all their free time on their hair, and guys who looked like they spent all their free time down at the acne farm. I saw young men who'd stop in the middle of the hall to do one-armed push-ups, and young men who'd scrawled "God Is Gay" in Whiteout on their backpacks.

But beneath all that, everyone at Stuy was *nice*. Even if they snarled and huffed, the seniors didn't beat you up. People mumbled, "Sorry" if they bumped into you in the halls; they said, "Excuse me" before charging past you on the stairs. Nobody went out of their way to bother you because everyone was incredibly self-motivated. The kids at Stuy cared about *their* grades, *their* problems. I fell quickly into that pattern.

Only a week into my freshman year, my train of thought was acting hyperactive. I'd be sprinting to class thinking, "Math, math, did you do it? Yeah, okay, what about English? Are you sure? Oh, wait: *lab!* No, lab's tomorrow, it's okay. . . ." I didn't have *time* to bother anyone else.

And no one else had time to bother me. I would've had to run through the halls naked, covered in chocolate sauce, for any seniors to acknowledge my presence. I came to view that as an advantage. I never had to worry about what others thought of me because they didn't think of me at all. They were concentrating on grades.

The Importance of Grades

Stuy gave number grades—84, 92, 100—instead of As and Bs. Every year, the administration talked about switching to a "nicer" grading system: letter grades of E, S, N, U (Excellent, Satisfactory, Needs Improvement, Unsatisfactory) or Pass/Fail. That never happened. Number grades made us work harder, and when we worked harder, we went to Good Colleges, and when we went to Good Colleges, the school's record looked great.

Grades were a touchy subject at Stuy. There was an etiquette about them. As they were handed out, you didn't turn to your friend and ask, "What are your grades?" You asked, "What'd you get?"—putting the blame for a potentially bad grade on the teacher. If you asked someone what he "got," you had to be ready to answer the same question yourself. If you saw someone visibly distraught over his grades, you didn't bug him—it was taboo. And you never, never bragged about what you got.

It was like a ballet, the intricate dance of the grades. Kids didn't bellow, "Seventy-five! You suck!" or "Yes! I got a ninety-eight!" But we were all *thinking* those things. We hid our celebration, gloating, and anguish, only revealing ourselves with subtle gestures: a slight smile, a clenched fist.

How the Cliques Operated

The constructive part of the Stuy grade obsession was that it distracted us from our social lives. When you're worrying about physics labs and *David Copperfield*, you don't have time to torture your peers. Stuy's student body wasn't vicious; it was simply separated into distinct groups that hoarded goods, traveled as one, and ostracized others.

First, we had the preppies. The preppies were okay; they had nice clothes, and they didn't smell bad. They all seemed to come from the same junior high school, and they recognized each other instantly on the first day. The girls were small and pretty, the guys well-built with great hair. The preppies always seemed busy, but you never really knew what they were up to. They would go off in little group—to eat? hang out? do drugs? have orgies? They'd come back from weekends with amazing stories (so-and-so got arrested, so-and-so performed this act upon so-and-so) that you could neither confirm nor deny. Generally, each preppy did one *non*-preppy thing to gain credibility, such as playing in a band or being a graffiti artist.

Speaking of artists, there were those, too: red-eyed, purple-haired poets, guys in turtlenecks, girls with hemp bracelets. These people loved seeing their names in obscure school magazines, and I was jealous of them because they were jaded. I wanted so badly to be jaded at Stuy. I wanted to walk around slumped over, mumbling cynically to myself, proving that even at age fourteen, I'd been there, done that.

There were the wanna-be Gen-Xers, too. Preppies with stubble, they had as much money as the rich kids but spent it on skateboards, cigarettes, Rollerblades, punk clothes, and hair dye. One of them wore a name tag that read, "Hello, My Name Is . . . Satan." Like the preppies, who congregated around a Snapple machine by the lobby, the wanna-be Gen-Xers had their own hangout: a small concrete ledge called "The Wall." They stayed out on The Wall during school, playing chess and exchanging snotty small talk.

Stuyvesant also had some great sports teams—in particular our swimming squad, the Penguins, won the city championships almost every year—so we had jocks. I didn't have much contact with them: they were quiet when they weren't hooting, and they generally kept to themselves. I had friends who became jocks, though. They would start the transformation over a period of weeks, spending more and more time after school with the team; then all of a sudden they'd be getting girlfriends and snazzy logo sweatshirts and talking to me in only the most cursory way.

A Clique of Bozos and Rejects

Behind the jocks, artists, nerds, preppies, chess nuts, heavy-metal guys, folksy guitar players, scary kids with black trench coats, neo-Nazis, and what's-his/her-names was the general collection of bozos and rejects that I hung out with. Most of them were Magic players—guys who spent their free time at Stuy playing a fantasy card game called *Magic: The Gathering.* We took over a corner of the sixth floor, where we sat on the ground with our cards. We came and went in shifts, playing during our lunch periods, running off to class as the bells rang. We couldn't really remember each other's names so we just yelled, "Hey you, you wanna play?" It was a desperate frenzy, kids playing *Magic* all the time, thinking about the cards so they wouldn't have to think about anything else.

I didn't only play *Magic*; between games, I befriended some computer people, some druggies, some music nuts, and some loners. The loners were interesting; they just walked around. No one teased them. No one really noticed them. They just . . . walked around.

Raising Girls Who Aren't Mean

Rosalind Wiseman

In 2001, Rosalind Wiseman published a New York Times *Magazine article titled "Mean Girls and the New Movement to Tame Them," where she discussed her work with teenage girls, teaching them how to stop engaging in cruel social behavior. After her article was published, hundreds of letters poured into the* New York Times *office from all over the world. She decided to follow her article with a book titled* Queen Bees and Wannabes, *which has become a standard text on the behavior of girls in cliques.*

In the following selection, Wiseman discusses her work with girls and their parents and offers advice to parents on how to handle the situations that arise, whether their daughters are victims of bullying or perpetrators.

We like to think that girls' cliques are worse today than they used to be, but I know that's not true. While writing the book [*Queen Bees and Wannabes*] I was struck by how universal an experience this seems to be, but it's a universal experience that no one talked about. I had 60- and 30-year-old women follow me around at parties to tell me about clique incidents as if they had just happened yesterday—all the girls' names are still right there. They told me about situations identical to the ones I'm working with right now. So yes, I think this kind of behavior has always been around. It may start a little younger than it used to. Girls are sexualized at a younger age and will deal with these friendship issues at a younger age too. I see 8-year-old girls, even 4-year-old girls, anointing certain friends and excluding others.

There are always going to be Queen Bees, even in the poorest schools. But typically the wealthier a community is, the more of a problem this is.

One thing that is worse today is how parents behave. I think that today's parents are either micromanaging their kids' lives or they are out of the picture, which is equally problematic. These kids will do anything to create space or get the appropriate attention.

But I disagree with some critics, who say worrying about clique behavior is micromanaging kids' social lives. Instead, I think every time you deal with one of these friendship issues it's a teaching moment about ethics. It's at these moments that your kids realize what you stand for.

How to Handle Girls' Cruelty

The whole issue of mean girls touches a nerve with parents, especially with mothers. Women are in such turmoil about how to raise assertive, strong women. Yet in our efforts to raise girls with high self-esteem, we sometimes lose sight of the importance of kindness. In schools I've worked in, I've seen girls with very high self-esteem who are really, really nasty.

As a parent, one of the hardest things to do is to decide how to handle these situations. Should you wade in, do nothing, or stand there and cheerlead, but let her fight for herself?

I think that unless a child is in a very serious situation, you should encourage her to stand up for herself, with her skills in place. By that I mean that parents should affirm their daughter and her courage, and then help her think through how to deal with the situation. Have her write it down, and decide what the most important issue is. The best strategy is usually for a girl to get the bully away from the other girls, describe to her what's happening, what she needs to happen differently, and have the bully affirm her.

In other words, parents should be their daughter's cheerleaders, but not take care of her business. If she can face this, she can face anything. Dealing with a girl bully will give her practice for someday having to deal with an inappropriate boss.

Talking About Problems

To let her know it's okay to tell you about clique problems, say something like, "Hey look, lots of times it's normal to have problems with friendships. If you ever have a problem with that, I'll help you or we can get you an ally, like an aunt or an older friend, to help you." Then you run away. Plant the seed and run away.

When do kids tell me they will reach out to their parents? The number one time is in the car while the parent is driving. Girls also tell me that if they try to get alone with their mom, it's usually because they need to talk. Even if they say it isn't a big deal, it is. They need at that moment to check in with her.

One final point about talking with girls. Sometimes parents ask questions that are actually springboards to asserting what they think or feel. They say, "How's it going with Amy?" because they want to say they don't like her. In cases like these, your daughter will shut down. Keep in mind that talking with her is not an opportunity to force-feed her your opinions.

Holding Teens Accountable

Unfortunately, it's really the exceptional parent who holds his or her child responsible for bad clique behavior. Recently I heard of a woman who found out that her daughter was behind all the nastiness going on in the girl's fifth grade class—the girl was totally the Queen Bee—and this mom believed the principal even though she was shocked. She talked to her kid and withdrew her privileges, which mostly meant taking away her means of communication—instant messaging and e-mail. And that really hurts a girl that age. But sadly, I've found that it's rare for most parents to hold their kids accountable for these unacceptable behaviors.

The hardest work for me is dealing with a Queen Bee girl and a Queen Bee mom. Those operating from a position of privilege don't like to be told they should change, nor do they believe there really is a problem. It's the kids on the outside who know the most about a school's social hierarchy.

Over and over again I have been struck by parents' unwillingness to apologize to other parents for their kids' behavior. It really hurts parents' relationships with each other at the worst possible time. Kids may start lying to you when they're teens, and if those parent friendships dry up, you'll be cut off from knowing what's going on, making it harder for you to keep your own girl safe.

The bottom line? Affirm her and hold her accountable. If your girl does something mean, she's not necessarily a mean person and you're not a bad parent.

When Cliques Get Mixed Up

Katherine Gorham

Mix It Up at Lunch Day is a project formulated by the Southern Poverty Law Center's Teaching Tolerance Program with the idea that if young people can learn to spend some time with those outside their normal cliques they might make new friends and break down barriers between groups. The organization has implemented Mix It Up days across America. The students at most schools have been surprised by how much they enjoy breaking out of their normal routines, but some schools have recorded that students disliked the concept and cooperated reluctantly.

A student named Katherine Gorham led a Mix It Up at Lunch Day at her school on September 10, 2007. In the following essay, she explains how she prepared for the event and was able to make it work successfully.

When my art teacher and community service coordinator handed me a Mix It Up pamphlet, I immediately fell in love with the program. At first, I'd thought of forming a "welcoming committee" to try and help kids become friends, but after reading about Mix It Up, I knew this was the program to follow.

The "welcoming committee" immediately became the Mix It Up club. I paired up with my best friend Nina, who also showed an interest in "mixing it up," and together we tried to get others involved. We held meetings almost every other week, but consistently, no one showed up. I ordered the beginner's packet with the stickers and posters, and together my best friend and I tried to raise awareness of the program. Still, no one showed up to the meetings.

With the help of three teachers who were very passionate about the club, Nina and I set out on our own to make Mix It

Katherine Gorham, "I Kept Thinking of Things That Could Go Wrong," Teaching Tolerance, www.tolerance.org, November 10, 2008. Reproduced by permission.

Up at Lunch Day a success. We hung up the posters, handed out stickers and told everyone to "mix it up!" Sooner or later almost everyone in the school knew something about Mix It Up at Lunch Day.

Despite the growing interest, Nina and I still struggled with meetings because no one was showing up. But with reassuring words from my art teacher, we kept working at it. I didn't give up. I knew it was important. Our school has so many cliques that no one wants to leave their own groups, not even for a lunch period. Many people don't think there is a problem at our school because they all belong to their own cliques.

However, some minority students prove them wrong. One girl who takes the city bus to school everyday said that she was "afraid because [she] thought that no one would sit with [her]." Also, last year we had a new girl come to our school. She was constantly picked on for two weeks until it came to a point where she threw a girl into a desk and gave her a concussion. The new girl was arrested and no one has seen her since. No one has really forgotten about that event—at least I haven't. Today, school violence, drugs and alcohol continue to be problems. So, with these incidents in mind, and with the wise words of our teachers in mind, I knew that I had to do this whether it worked or not.

When the big day was less than a week away, many people began to talk about it. Everyone was saying, "Oh, that's the stupidest idea ever. No one's going to move!" The day before the lunch was scheduled, I presented in front of the student council, and they all agreed to take part and support the new Mix It Up club. They felt it was their responsibility. At a faculty meeting that same day, the teachers agreed to help out as well, with the majority of teachers promising to stay in the cafeteria during our Mix event.

Preparing for the Event

I signed up for a speaker and microphone and burned a Mix It Up CD with upbeat songs. I also stayed two hours after school painting huge signs to hang up in the lobby and cafeteria. One of the signs read, "Mix it Up Graffiti Board," and had a space where people wrote what they thought about the event.

I have to admit, I haven't been more nervous about any event in my life than I was about lunch on Tuesday. I didn't get any sleep the night before because I kept thinking of things that could go wrong the next day. Even Nina kept saying, "I just don't think that anyone is going to move." Not having my best friend on my side was discouraging.

Finally, the day arrived. With the help of some teachers and janitors, we moved all of the tables in the cafeteria so no one could find their regular seat. This was important because when everyone came into the cafeteria, they had to sit somewhere different because they had no choice. While walking down to the cafeteria with a microphone in hand, I thought I was going to faint. I set up a speaker, stood on a chair and began to talk in front of about 150 kids. I said:

"Today we are all taking part in a national event. This is Mix It Up at Lunch Day, and all across the U.S. thousands of kids, including us, are switching seats at lunch. So for this period, sit with someone you have never talked to before and make a new friend. And when lunch is over, come and sign the Mix It Up Graffiti Board. Have fun and *Mix it up!*"

When I finished speaking and stepped down, to my surprise, many kids began to get up and move! After the first lunch period was over, I began to hear, "Oh I wish I thought to sit there," and such, which gave me the idea to remind kids about what to do as they came into the cafeteria. So for the second and third lunch periods, I was up on my chair with Nina next to me and we took turns telling kids to switch seats as they came flowing in. This worked much better because everyone made more of an effort to find somewhere new to sit.

The Result Was Surprising

I was astonished at the kids I saw sitting together. All the cliques were blended in! After I saw everyone situated with new people, I sat at a different table myself and met some new friends. Throughout the lunch periods, the teachers went around encouraging kids to move. They played a huge role in making lunch successful. They stood at the doors when kids came in and said, "Find a different seat!"

After taking down the graffiti sign, I couldn't believe how many people wrote on it and what they wrote on it. People wrote:

- "I thought that I wouldn't like it, but I really did!"

- "It was a great idea!"

- "We should do this every week!"

- "Next time, to make it better, you should do this . . ."

- "I never thought that I would ever like talking to this person."

At the same time there were a few haters, but I wasn't surprised. I actually thought there would have been more people saying how they hated it. In the hallways I heard people talking about who they sat with and how they should hang out with those kids more. People kept coming up to me saying how much they loved it. Having a successful Mix It Up Day has been one of the greatest successes in my life and I just cannot wait until Nina and I do it again next year.

SOCIAL ISSUES
FIRSTHAND

CHAPTER 2

Victims and Perpetrators

I Was Bullied Because
I Was Different

Steve M.

In the following selection, teenager Steve M. details the bullying and torment that began in elementary school because he was different. Steve had to wear leg braces, and he remembers that no one could quite understand his pain. Now, he looks back on those years with a different perspective as he gains confidence in himself.

My hell is a bit different from how mythologies or religions depict it. My hell is Hadfield Elementary School.

Elementary school is perhaps the most vicious, ruthless, unaccepting atmosphere that exists on this planet. The groups, the cliques, the gangs are unstoppable and unbearable. At least it seems that way from the outside. It's almost a twisted caste system—you are labeled when you start school, and there is no deviation from it, no matter how much you may change. Cool kids are cool kids, dirty kids are dirty kids, dorks are dorks. Forever.

And different is wrong. If you are different you are wrong, and therefore are punished verbally, physically and mentally. But I guess I couldn't say that I wasn't different. I was quite different, in fact. But to be crucified simply because of physical differences, and to have an atmosphere that basically supports that, is a terrible thing to which to subject children. The very qualities that are supposed to be so genuine in children—love, trust, innocence, acceptance—were nowhere to be found in my elementary school. It made me believe that acceptance is a quality to gain, not one that one is born with and loses in time.

My style of the day was a perfect match for a dodge-ball target. I had the excellent stereotypical dork-kid physique, and then some. I sported a nifty bowl cut (which ran for 12 years), glasses, over-the-ear hearing aids (the "my grandma has those" kind), a few extra pounds, and from ages five to seven, a set of leg braces à la Forrest Gump. I was the perfect target. The perfect target. [Case in point:] I had an entire 14-page joke book written about my lovely proportions and attachments, complete with songs (including one entitled "Muffin Man," which detailed my lunch-time routine), poems and much more.

In My Own World

But the leg braces were probably the worst part. Many things come with having a one-in-5,000,000 hip disease, but nothing compares to the loneliness. I'd come home and whine to my parents all I wanted about how much I got made fun of, how much I got pushed around and talked about behind my back, but they never really understood. No one really could. Being made fun of for being overweight or having glasses or not having money are things at least some can relate to, but I was in my own world.

There was no one who felt exactly the way I did. No one else viewed the world like a senile old man at the age of seven and hated everyone. I'm not going to say I got beat up every day and shoved in dumpsters, but I can guarantee you that during recess I found my own little spot in the bushes to cry. Actually, after all the words of hate I'd heard, a dip in the dumpster wouldn't have been all that bad compared to the verbal volleys.

For the time being, my life in elementary school was nothing but pure torture. A pain that never subsided. Weekends only added to the misery with countless hours alone with no one to call or play with. But that made it that much easier to accept everyone else.

I came out of elementary school, oddly, a much stronger, more confident person. Almost everyone I know now would describe me as outgoing (as well as ruggedly handsome), and that is something of which I'm very proud. When I entered middle school, I couldn't wait to meet new people and find some with whom I was comfortable. Of course, many of the elementary-school kids were still around, but I was able to find a group of close friends, many who had experienced the same type of elementary-school humiliation.

Today, when I see those I once feared so much, I feel nothing but confidence. I feel like David casting my shadow over a fallen Goliath, freed and relieved. Six years of pain seems infinitesimal compared with the incredible feeling of strength and freedom that now resides in me. And nothing can express my sentiments to my tormentors in elementary school quite like the Rice University chant can:

"It's alright, it's okay. You'll be working for me, anyway."

Labels and Slurs
Hurt Everyone

Aisha Muharrar

*Aisha Muharrar is a young African American woman who al-
ways loved to write and decided to pen* More Than Just a Label
*about a phenomenon she witnessed at her Long Island high
school. When people grouped into cliques and when they excluded or criticized others, often the behavior was accompanied
by labeling. Muharrar wrote about the problems that arise when
we approach each other—and think of ourselves—in such a re-
stricted way. In the section of the book that follows, Muharrar
discusses her experience with a particularly poisonous type of labeling—slurs and hate words.*

Okay, first things first. You may be wondering how a Long
Island teen like myself ends up writing a book about labels. Like so many high school experiences, it can all be traced
back to freshman year (for me, that was 1998–99). While
drifting off to sleep one night, I began to think about all the
different groups of teens in my high school. I had thought
about the social groups at my school and other high schools
around the nation before. It's hard not to notice that even
though labels may not always be said aloud, they're floating
around in the high school atmosphere.

That night was different, though. It had only been a few
months since the Columbine High School shootings. I was
fourteen, and the idea of teens murdering their peers appalled
me. I'm sure many other teens were thinking about that tragedy late at night, too.

After Columbine, it was difficult not to think about labels
and social groups. The media kept talking about how labels,

cliques, bullying, and the pressure to fit in were taking a toll on high school students everywhere. I couldn't help but think that if violence happened at Columbine and other schools, it could happen at any high school. When I later met and talked to two students from Littleton, Colorado (where Columbine High School is), it became even clearer to me that they were just like teens everywhere in America.

Taking Action to Prevent Violence

I decided to start an anti-violence committee at my high school in tenth grade. I wanted to help maintain the relatively peaceful environment in my school and educate others about how violence erupts. While working on this committee, I corresponded with a national anti-violence/pro-tolerance organization known as SHiNE. I was the volunteer youth reporter for one of their charity benefits—a really cool concert held by New York radio station Z100, featuring performances by Jennifer Lopez and Smashmouth.

So, I was already interested in preventing violence and promoting respect before I wrote this book. I kept thinking about labels and their role in high school life. I never believed that labels were the sole reason for Columbine—not for a second. But I did understand that labels played a part. I wanted to do something. And I knew that writing was the key.

The summer before my junior year started with a bang. I was selected to be a member of *Teen People*'s News Team. For those of you who may not know, *Teen People* is the youth version of *People* magazine. Each year, *Teen People* announces the search for teens to write articles for the magazine. I applied twice. When I was thirteen, I was rejected; but the second time, I had to send a brief description of myself and a writing sample, and I submitted the article I'd written for SHiNE. I was thrilled when *Teen People* picked me.

As a News Team correspondent, I got to go to the magazine's offices and meet the other teen writers. It was great to get to know such unique and interesting teens from all parts of the country and Canada. Plus, I was published a few times. Maybe you saw my work?

Labels at My School

In school, I was still doing what most teens do, hanging out and studying. And I was still thinking about labels. Every time I saw someone get snubbed or teased, I thought more about labels, cliques, and other social dividers at my school. I was friends with a variety of teens who had a variety of labels: one was called a goth, some were called preps and others nerds, some were called freaks. I tended to ignore the social labels and talk to people I liked. But I didn't think it was right that there were all these groups in the first place.

The labels didn't matter much to me, but I noticed they mattered to others. My friends in one group often would make fun of my friends in another. No matter how popular or unpopular the group was, there was some other group it didn't want to associate with or tried to avoid. Why didn't they like each other? Some didn't even know each other—they based their opinions solely on labels. I understood, though, that labels never gave the full picture. I couldn't have described each friend with just one label—so how could other people do it so easily?

I was frustrated by the unspoken rules that seemed to govern high school life. To me, the labels that people gave each other—or themselves—were like invisible name tags. Once you started to "wear" one, everyone was free to make assumptions about who you are.

I began to ask myself questions about teens and labeling. Who actually hands out these labels? What role do the labels play? Do they help or harm? Do people like their labels? Do they hate them? Are they even aware of them? What's the truth behind all these labels? That's what I wanted to find out. . . .

What About Hate Words?

When I first came up with the idea to write a book about labels, I planned to focus on the social labels that are common today—geek, stoner, teen queen, jock. But in the surveys, many teens said that racial, religious, or sexual hate words were their personal labels. To me, these aren't *labels*. I believe that names intended to insult a person's race, religion, or sexuality are slurs.

Slurs are hate words like nigger, dyke, cracker, white trash, chink, gook, flip, JAP, kike, faggot, flamer, queer, bitch, whore, ghetto, towelhead, Jesus freak, gimp, crip, and retard, for a start. This makes for some stomach-churning reading for most people. If the Teen Labels Survey is any guide, teens are exposed to all of these slurs and more all the time.

Slurs attack the core of who you are—the fundamental you. These hate words aren't based on the clothes you wear or the friends you hang out with. The words cut down *who* you are and *how* you are: your immutable identity.

Slurs are worse than labels—much worse. These words hurt more deeply because they show contempt for things you can't change about yourself: the sex you were born, your skin color, your sexual orientation, being in a wheelchair, having dyslexia, your first language, or the religion you've been raised in. It's very painful to have the core of your identity or aspects of your individuality attacked in these ways.

Slurs can be used to target anyone: Individuals and groups. Girls and guys. African Americans, Asians, Latinos, Arabs, Caucasians, Native Americans, Pacific Islanders, and people of mixed race. Gays, lesbians, bisexuals, and transgender teens. People with disabilities. Catholics, Protestants, Jews, Mormons, Muslims, Hindus, and Sikhs. People perceived as being one of the above. Do you see yourself anywhere on this list? I do.

What Happened to Me

I've had my own experiences with slurs, and one instance really sticks out in my mind. In junior high, I went to a

Valentine's dance with a group of friends. I was hanging out at Barry's table; he was one of the most popular boys in school at the time, and I thought it was pretty cool to be sitting with him. We were having fun, and I was enjoying myself. Then another boy picked up a candy bar off the floor and was going to eat it. Barry began arguing with him, saying the candy bar wasn't clean. I was surprised. Barry was popular, but he wasn't known for his hygiene (none of the seventh grade boys were).

And then Barry blurted out: "Don't touch that. A nigger could have touched it." I felt my world stop as soon as the word left his mouth. I was stunned and shocked. I had just been laughing and goofing around a few moments earlier. Now the dance was ruined for me. Yet, I said nothing. Where was my sharp rebuttal? To this day, I don't know why Barry said what he said or why I remained silent.

I heard Barry whisper, "She didn't hear me. She didn't hear me." His attempts to cover his actions were pitiful. Everyone knew I had heard him. I whispered to my friend that we should go. We got up, and as soon as we were out of earshot, I began to cry. No one came to my defense; no one apologized.

Maybe you've had your own experiences with hateful words and the weight they carry. Even if the words were used in a supposed joke, and even if the person who used them said, "I didn't mean anything by it," you probably felt hurt, angry, scared, or offended. Who wouldn't?

It's true that slurs are only words, and words don't have power unless you give them power. Still, hate speech generally does what it's intended to do—it makes you feel hated. It takes a very strong person to stand up to that kind of talk. Looking back, I wish I would have stood up for myself at the Valentine's dance, but I was so shocked at the time. Even though Barry hadn't directly called me that slur, I should have told him not to use the word at all.

I often wondered what would have happened if I were Caucasian and had heard Barry's comment. Because it wouldn't have been directed toward me, would I still be hanging out with Barry—even if I felt offended by what he said? What if, that night, Barry had made a derogatory comment about any other ethnic group and I'd overhead that instead? What would I have done? I know I never would have laughed, but would I have stayed friends with Barry and all those other people? Would I have kept quiet, like all the others did, and let him get away with that?

I Wanted to Fit In So Badly

Anonymous

In 2002, journalist Rachel Simmons wrote a book titled Odd Girl Out *about the "silent and indirect aggression" that girls use against one another. After its publication, she asked girls to send their personal stories to her, making the request at book signings and speeches, and posting a flyer on her Web site. Hundreds of responses flowed in. Simmons collected them in* Odd Girl Speaks Out.

The following piece by an eighteen-year-old young woman relates the story of her high school years, during which she never really fit into either of the two cliques that dominated the social scene at her school. Consequently, she was treated miserably.

All of my life, I have never really, truly "fit in." I was never really part of a group. My family never really had the money to buy me all of the clothing that was "in style." However, I still managed and I loved my school. At the end of sixth grade it closed, forcing me to go to another school, to make another desperate attempt to "fit in."

I was the only new girl to come to seventh grade at school. There were about eleven or twelve of us seventh-grade girls including me, and they were in two cliques. There were three really popular girls, and the semi-popular girls were all the rest. Our class was a mixture of both eighth graders and seventh graders, which made it even tougher because all the girls in eighth grade saw me as a loser, too.

Brittany, who was very popular and pretty, drew a picture when a substitute was in. It was a picture of the substitute naked, and she was quick to show the teacher and say that I drew it. I always got into trouble for pitiful little things such as these. I was an overweight girl, very shy and timid.

Things never got really bad until eighth grade. I suffered all of the time. All of the other girls had numerous boyfriends. They talked about all the sexual things that they had done with them. I had never been with a boy, had a boyfriend, or even considered having one. I was never invited to the birthday parties or the little girl get-togethers they would have every other day.

I was teased about everything: my clothes, my hair, my weight, my long face, the fact that I had no boobs. Often I would just go home and cry. It seemed like the only way to ease the pain. I considered suicide but never actually went through with it.

It was between these tough times that my mother and I had gotten very close. We became like the best of friends. While I was dealing with all of the torment and taunting, I was having problems with my teacher. So I went to school and came home every day crying about how so-and-so had said this, and how I thought this so-and-so was my best friend, how could they betray me like that?

It Just Kept Getting Worse

All of this teasing that I had already gone through was nothing compared to what was to come. I remember being at school in the computer lab one day, and this guy Nick asked me if I had said something about my cousin and how she had f---ed her boyfriend or something. I responded no.

Later on that week, the girls from my class wanted me to go to a dance. I found this odd, considering they never wanted me to do anything with them or even be near them. However, I said "okay." I wanted to fit in so badly. I didn't care.

Later on that night, I went into my closet and dug out my size thirteen formfitting jeans. I put them on and watched as my flab tumbled over the top of them. I put on my playgirl sweater, went into the bathroom, and put on some heavy makeup. I looked like a fat slut, but I didn't see it.

When I walked out of the bathroom, my mother told me to take off those jeans and go put on my wind-breakers. She could see that it wasn't me. I never did like the tight formfitting clothes. However, I got pissed off at her and refused to talk to her, I was so bent on going to this dance and looking good.

It even got to the point where she told me that she would not allow me to leave the house until I at least changed my pants. When we began to leave and go to the dance, she dropped me off in front of the hall. I got out, still refusing to talk to her, and she said, "Call me if you want to leave earlier, I love you." Still I did not answer her. I quickly went inside and found all of the girls whom I had considered to be my friends standing there.

Things Aren't as They Seem

They all embraced me saying, "Hey there, I'm so happy that you could come." Moments afterward, a girl named Marie and my cousin confronted me.

Marie began to swear and curse at me saying things like, "You f---ing fat bitch! Starting shit 'bout ma girl Randi here!" She went on forever, and not one person, not one, helped me. I stood there on the verge of tears, not saying anything, feeling betrayed and angered. Marie threatened me a few times and then walked away saying she was going to get her friends to kick my ass.

At that moment, I ran, scared shitless of what they might do to me, knowing that no one was ever going to help me. I ran out of the dance hall crying, I ran a long, dark mile. I got to the nearest country-style donut shop where I knew some people. I went to a pay phone, called my mom, and broke down into tears. My mom quickly came and got me. I embraced her, shaking, terrified, and crying so hard that I was barely even able to get the words out of my mouth. She hugged me and we sat there in that parking lot for an hour.

We came home, and my mom called my cousin's mother. She instantly began to side with Randi, saying that I had always been backward and blah blah blah. Randi had done nothing, all that her mom could see was her sweet little angel who she let do whatever the hell she wanted to.

School Became Impossible

The next day I went to school, and as I walked in, I was told by one of the popular girls to "leave, like seriously, just die." I thought she was joking, as she was known as the drama queen, so I laughed. But then when everyone was staring at me I realized, Oh my god, she's serious. I ran inside and cried again.

I made myself sick in the bathroom so that I could come home. Once I told my mom, she kept me home from school for a week. When I went back I got the same looks and curses from the same people. I was an outcast, and everyone around our little town knew my name, for a bad reason. A majority wanted to kick my ass.

I began to feel really insecure about myself. I went on a diet thinking, maybe if I'm thin they will like me. I began losing weight, first twenty pounds, then thirty pounds. By graduation, I had gone down from a size thirteen to a nine. I was very proud of myself. I had gone from 178 pounds and 5'5" to 148 pounds.

The others around me continued to be unimpressed. Since the rumors, I hadn't talked to anyone. I would not leave my house or talk on the phone. I was scared. After school was over, I was so happy. I lost more weight in the summer and I grew, too. By the end of the summer, I was around 5'7" and 121 pounds. When I went back to my dietitian, she said that this was unhealthy, and that I needed to stop dieting because I was very underweight. She gave me exercises to do so that I might be able to build some muscle.

Finding Peace with Myself

Now I sit at a happy 142 pounds. My friends tell me I look great, and I do feel it. I'm so proud of myself. I have true friends now that I just couldn't bear to live without. They keep me going. They are a big part of me and who I am. My marks [grades] are doing fine. I still don't have a boyfriend, but I really don't have the desire to have one anymore. Since I go to high school in another town, I stay with my new friends as much as possible.

I am still scared of my hometown and the people in it. But I have left them behind because they don't matter anymore. I'm me. I'm not tiny, I'm not the most beautiful person in the world, but I'm me and that's all that I can be. And even though the past will continue to haunt me and will scar me for life, I know in my heart my friends will always be there to help me through it. I can't believe it. Oh my god, I have friends.

What I Did to Be Popular

Demi Chang

Sometimes the desperation to belong forces someone to do something she never thought she would do. In the following selection, Demi Chang recalls a high school incident in which she betrays a good friend to gain entrance into a popular clique. She finds out that popularity is not at all what she expected.

I wished it had never happened. I wished I had never done what I did. I look back in time and think of how foolish I was. I remember what happened clear as day, replaying it over and over in my mind. In my mind I would change the events. Instead of going along with the scheme, I would say "no" and walk away. But that's not what really happened, and as I hard as I try, I can't change the past.

At the beginning of the school year I was a new transfer student. I dressed plainly and always tied my hair back. I had no extravagant clothes, wore no makeup. Let's face it—with my look no one was going to notice me.

Over the course of my first few months I gained a true friend. She introduced herself to me the first day I was in school, and we had eaten lunch together ever since. We talked about everything and trusted each other with our deepest, darkest secrets. In only two short months we were like sisters and did everything together. We often joked about what it would be like being the most popular girls in school and how it would be so cool to have everyone love us. I had seen the girls who were popular, and they were gorgeous. Perfect hair, teeth, skin, smiles, and most of all, perfect lives. From the outside, they had it all.

A Chance to Be Popular

Then, a week before winter recess, the most popular girl in school, Rachel, came up to me in the hallway and pulled me into the empty locker room. At first, I wondered if she thought I was someone else. She had the usual girls and boys trailing behind her and they were all looking excited. I didn't know what was going on, but I just went along with it.

"Hi. You're Jenny's best friend, right?" she asked, obviously knowing the answer. I nodded, still wondering what this was all about. "I'm offering you the chance of a lifetime. When an opportunity like this presents itself, it's always smart to seize it. Am I right?" she asked the boys and girls behind her. They all murmured in agreement. Big surprise.

"I'm offering you a chance to be one of us. You will be standing next to me, talking, chatting, smiling and flipping your hair with me in the hallways and anywhere we go. You will be popular. You will be loved. You have potential, and with the right help, you could be one of us." Her eyes blazed as she said this.

This was my chance! This was what I had been dreaming of! It was obvious there was going to be a catch, but I didn't care. This was going to be the best day of my life. Or so I thought.

"Now. All you have to do is tell me one of Jenny's secrets and we'll start the makeover during winter break." She said it so casually that I knew she was hiding something.

"Why?" I questioned.

"Because, we're going to spread it around the school like wildfire and make it the rumor of the year."

She explained that Jenny's boyfriend from the drama club was the guy Rachel liked. (Who knew that Rachel didn't like jocks like most cheerleaders?) Of course it wasn't Jenny's fault, but at the time, apparently with only dust in my head, I thought Jenny was horrible. I convinced myself that Jenny must have known that Rachel liked this boy and dated him out of spite. Bottom line—what I thought *most* about was me being popular. Pathetic, I know.

So I agreed. I agreed because I wanted that taste of popularity. I agreed because I was now cold in the heart with selfish greed. I agreed and became one of them. Over that winter's break I was changed into someone completely different. Hair, makeup, clothes, even my personality.

No Real Friends

When winter recess was over, I proudly walked into school by Rachel's side. I felt bolder, like I was on top of the world. And it felt great right until Jenny snatched my arm and screamed, "How could you?" She rambled on about true friendship and betrayal for another thirty seconds before Rachel pulled me away.

"Do we know you, loser?" Rachel asked as she flipped her hair and we started to walk away. I turned to see Jenny's eyes filled with hate. Then my heart started to sink. I felt horrible. But I soon forgot when everyone started crowding around me, chatting constantly. *This isn't bad*, I thought. Compliments filled my head, and soon I even became more popular than Rachel. Everyone loved me, but what good was that?

Weeks later, I had no *real* friends. I had people follow me like dogs, not friends. I mean, where were my "friends" when I was feeling down? Where were they when I needed someone to talk to? They were only around to shop and to make me look popular.

I passed Jenny occasionally in the hallway. She never looked at me once. She now had a new best friend who was definitely a better friend considering how disgustingly I had treated her. Being loyal was what being a true friend was all about. I trashed that and walked all over it.

Yeah, being popular was all I ever wanted, but who knew that behind all the smiles were cold, empty hearts? So *this* was what it was like to be truly popular. I still remember those days when Jenny and I would talk on the phone constantly and laugh and joke about silly things. Where was that now? It had disappeared, just like my true identity. I hid all the things I wanted to say and smiled as if everything was always okay. What was I now? Sure, being popular was cool at the beginning, but after the initial excitement, where was this going to take me? Nowhere. I wished I could take back all that I did. I was rude and mean, and most of all I lost my only true friend. Actions have consequences, and mine were the worst of all. I lost my true happiness and settled for a cold, meaningless existence. For the next year in school, I lived miserably, a smile plastered to my face.

Now life is different. I have learned greatly from my mistake of choosing social acceptance over a true friend. I would never betray a friend again after what I have done. I've met new people, made new friends. Some people still regard me as the one who changed drastically and became popular, but that's all behind me now. My new friends are truly the best that I can ever have, and we are closer than anything in the world. We love each other for who we are, not by our social status in school. Nothing will ever tear us apart. Not even an opportunity of rising to the top because, let's face it, even the top isn't as great as everyone says it is.

The Boy I Should Have Dated

Camryn Green

Camryn Green passed up the chance of romantic involvement with an unpopular boy at her school. Because he was part of a clique she didn't want to be associated with, she limited their relationship to a platonic friendship. In this selection, as Green looks back, she regrets her narrow-mindedness.

There was one boy named Elliot who was in my classes. He was a smart kid. I would call him almost every night to help me with my homework. We went through algebra, trigonometry, and calculus together. We laughed a lot on the phone, making fun of our teachers. We talked about the books *Siddhartha* and *Steppenwolf*. We talked about our parents. But I never ever considered him a potential boyfriend.

Even though he was fun on the phone, Elliot was basically a nerd. He was short, he wore white socks, had braces, played the oboe—and got good grades.

I also got good grades. But for some strange reason, I tried to keep that a secret from my friends. I never let on that I studied. But Elliot knew. In fact, we sometimes studied together.

Nowhere to Belong

My boyfriend was the star basketball player. I had friends in lots of different crowds. I hung out with the jocks because my boyfriend was one. But I wasn't a jock.

I also hung out with the hippies because my friend, Jan, was one. But I wasn't really a hippie. I sometimes hung out with the theater people. But I wasn't a theater person. Everyone thought I was popular—but really I didn't feel part of any crowd.

There was only one crowd I didn't want to be part of. The nerd crowd.

One day Elliot called me. His parents were having an anniversary party and he was supposed to bring somebody. He wanted to know if I wanted to come.

I didn't want to go with him. But I didn't want to hurt his feelings. I finally told Elliot no. I can still remember how I did it. I passed him a note in English class. I was a coward.

And even though he still helped me with my homework afterwards, his voice was a little quieter when we talked, we laughed less.

In senior year, I spent less time with my boyfriend who was now in community college. Elliot went out with a girl who was a sophomore. I'd see them walking down the halls, holding hands. I felt a twinge of jealousy when I saw them.

Things Don't Turn Out as Expected

When I went to college, Elliot went to college nearby. The basketball player and I broke up. It was Elliot who I talked to about Jungian psychology. Elliot who I spoke to about my dreams. Elliot who I talked to about my fears about being fat when I gained the famous freshman 15.

But when he came to visit me, I wasn't physically attracted to him. I still thought of him as having braces, being short, and wearing white socks.

He started dating somebody in college and so did I. By the time we met again, it was 10 years later. He had invited me to his wedding. He was over 6 feet tall, with a long beard and piercing blue eyes. He was studying for his Ph.D.

I was attracted to him. I admit it. I was jealous. I could have had him, even for a short time, I could have been with him. Together. And now it was too late.

When I think now of the people who weren't popular in high school, I think of people like Elliot, who went on to become a professor of comparative religion, write a best-selling book, and earn minor celebrity with an appearance on Oprah.

And I think of my basketball player boyfriend. I heard recently that he was divorced and cleaning houses in Florida.

Being One of the Nasty Girls

Alice Wong

In this selection, Alice Wong writes about how it feels to be part of a clique that is known for being critical of others. In middle school she became attached to a popular, mean clique—one in which she did not fit, but the task of finding new friends was daunting. When she became a victim of her own clique's exclusion, she found comfort in some new, caring friends.

At the end of eighth grade, my classmates and I hung around after school signing each other's yearbooks. After my classmate Diana signed mine, I noticed she'd written, "Thank you for getting me into the gossip group."

I was shocked. I felt horrible. I didn't want people to associate me with a group labeled "the gossip group."

But, the sad thing was, the girls in that gossipy group had been my closest friends for much of junior high. I don't know which I felt worse about—that I'd been part of their clique or that they'd kicked me out of it.

I met the members of my clique—Maggie, Marsha, Kayla, and Bethany—in sixth grade, the first year of junior high school. They were friendly and outgoing, and they helped me meet some new friends too—which I liked, since I was shy.

I was also naïve and thought everyone was kind. I thought my new friends were funny. They talked to me about their problems and I confided in them. They seemed to fill all the qualities I was looking for in friends.

My friends were also striving to be popular, and as the semester progressed, they got what they wanted. People in school knew who they were. For me, being part of the popular group was okay, but it wasn't as important as being accepted by a group.

Belonging to the Wrong Clique

But during that year, I also began to notice changes in their personalities. They seemed to think that being popular meant putting everyone else down.

Kayla was the leader of the group. People wouldn't know whether or not the rest of us agreed with what she said because we were robots. We went along with her even if our own opinions were different.

One day, Kayla pointed at an eighth grader in the hall and commented loudly on "what a big nose" he had. The group laughed, but I didn't. I thought it was rude.

Another time, Kayla kept pointing at some guy and laughing. I didn't see anything funny about him, but the rest of the clique did. They noticed his crooked teeth. They tended to notice all the little things about a person, things I didn't focus on when I saw someone.

They loved to label people "dorky" or "geeky." They gossiped about how people acted or what they'd heard about them through friends and acquaintances.

I often thought about what would happen if I told them how I felt when they were mean, but I was afraid to because I didn't want to lose their friendship. I was used to them and thought it would be too difficult to get to know a new group of people.

I was also afraid that if I spoke up, they'd all turn on me as well. I'd already had a taste of how it would feel to have their cruelty aimed at me.

One of the girls in the group, Bethany, had a particularly mean attitude and sometimes put me down like she did people outside our group. One day, I was wearing a name-brand shirt and she came over to check the label.

"Is that real?" she said in a very obnoxious and loud tone as she peered and tugged on the back of my shirt. Everyone just stared. My cheeks turned red from embarrassment.

She knew I wasn't the type who'd confront her, so she took advantage of my weakness. I felt hurt and angry that other members of the group did nothing to stick up for me.

I was beginning to really dislike my friends. But I still wanted to be part of their group.

Becoming a Victim

When eighth grade began, I hung with the clique during lunch and before and after school, but I also started to make new friends. I met people like Eva and Melissa in different classes, and I could talk to them about things like our favorite bands and how we liked to sing and write poetry—things my old friends couldn't have cared less about.

Whenever I was with my new friends and saw the girls in my clique, it was awkward. I usually didn't introduce them to each other because I didn't think the girls in my clique would be interested in meeting them.

Then one day, about three months before eighth grade ended, I sat down at my clique's usual lunch table. The clique was late, so I waited for them alone. After a few minutes, they came. Marsha and Maggie said hi, but Bethany and Kayla said nothing.

I didn't know why they were acting so distant toward me, but I thought if I just left it alone, they'd get over whatever was bothering them. So I went to where some of my other friends were sitting and chatted with them for a while.

When I came back to the clique's table, Kayla gave me this stare. I knew something was very wrong indeed. She said she had something to discuss with Marsha and didn't want me to listen to the conversation. I was like, "Okay," but felt left out.

I went to chat with my friend Jacqueline, who was sitting in the far corner of the lunchroom, but in the back of my mind I kept wondering what was up with the clique.

A few minutes later, the bell rang. On my way to the exit, Kayla called me over to the table. She told me that she didn't like that I associated with friends outside the clique. She said that if I wanted to remain in the group, I had to follow their rules. She didn't exactly say she wanted me out of the group, but it was obvious from her expression that she did.

The rest of the group just stared in silence at us. They already knew what she was going to say and do. Kayla snickered while she talked to me. She was having fun rejecting me.

I was shocked, and then, as her words sank in, it really started to hurt. For the rest of the day, I tried avoiding her. I felt like crying, but I didn't want to show her how badly her words hurt me.

When I got home, my mom saw how troubled I looked and asked, "What's wrong?"

"Not much. I just have a lot on my mind."

I didn't feel like talking. I was very upset. But Mom was persistent. I finally spilled my guts.

She said things would get better. She assured me that everyone has problems like these, and I should accept that that's just how those girls were and that I couldn't change them. The only person I could change was myself.

But even though I'd known for a long time that they were mean to others, I couldn't accept that they'd been so cruel to me. I already missed them, because I'd been a part of their group for so long.

For weeks, I didn't have much of a social life. I kept to myself during school. I didn't hang with anyone after school. I wasn't up to doing anything fun. I was too upset. All I wanted was to be alone and have time to think everything through.

I even lost my appetite. My mother prepared my favorite dishes, like barbecued spareribs and fried noodles, but I only ate small portions.

New, Loyal Friends

The way my friends turned on me made me feel like I couldn't trust anyone. I began analyzing everything the girls in the clique had said to me. I felt like I should've figured out how Kayla and Bethany were going to treat me before it was too late. I was scared that if I were open with my new friends, they'd wind up hurting me too.

But, noticing I was blue, my new friends emailed me jokes and poems to try to brighten my mood. At first, I was too upset to find the jokes funny. But after a few days, I reread their emails and they made me laugh.

One Saturday, Eva and Melissa dragged me out to the park to play basketball, twirl on the balance beams, and ride our bikes. Then we went out for lunch. I had so much fun. I began to realize who my true friends were.

Still, it wasn't until the end of the summer that I really started to feel better. Thankfully, making new friends wasn't that difficult.

I realized I should've left the old clique once I knew how they were instead of waiting until they forced me out. I'm glad I'm no longer part of that group. If I was, I might've become as closed-minded as they were and missed out on the opportunity to meet new people.

I still feel guilty for the years I was a friend to those girls. Even though I didn't do most of the mean things they did, I continued to be a part of their group.

I'm still cool with the other friends I made in eighth grade. And when I went to high school, I was relieved to find that most people were much more respectful toward each other than in my junior high.

I started associating with all sorts of people who were friendly and kind. I didn't care anymore if I fit into any one group.

Now I realize that being in a clique doesn't determine my worth. When I was in the clique, people in and out of the group saw me as naïve, and I was close-minded to new people. Now people see me as an outgoing, friendly, and kind person, which is a more accurate reflection of who I am and want to be.

Abandoning a Member of the Clique

John Nikkah

During his graduate studies in clinical psychology at the New School for Social Research in New York City, John Nikkah published a collection of short pieces by young men titled Our Boys Speak: Adolescent Boys Write About Their Inner Lives. *In his introductory comments to the chapter on friendship, Nikkah tells a story about his own experiences in high school as part of a popular clique and his regrettable betrayal of a friend.*

We were known as the posse. We thought we were so cool and, more important, we knew that everyone else thought the same. We'd worked very hard to arrive at this favorable consensus. We threw all the best parties. We dated none but the most sought-after girls. We hung out only with those whom we deemed worthy of our attention. Interaction with classmates outside of our social circle was to be avoided at all costs. We adhered to every stereotype of the elitist high school clique, and I'm sorry to say that, yes, we *were* proud of our behavior. In high school, as in life, it often seems that the higher the walls between your group and others, the more self-important you and yours feel. I bought into this insanity all the way until the second semester of my senior year, when I found out what my "friends" were capable of.

Out of all the guys I was friends with in high school, I'd known Adam the longest. Freshman year, he was one of the most popular kids at school. His older brother was a social giant and nepotism cast a strong spell over the student body, raising Adam several notches above the average cool freshman in the general esteem. If the legacy factor wasn't enough, Adam had been blessed with yet another distinguishing characteristic. He was a year older than everyone in our grade—that's right, a freshman with a driver's license. While our fifteen-year-old contemporaries were cruising with Mom in the family truckster, or worse yet, suffering the indignity of regulation yellow school district transit, Adam's friends were always sitting pretty. Adam had celebrity status at my high school; people would feel honored just to walk down a hall with him during school hours. So when he introduced me to his friends in the cool crowd, I thought that my standing atop the uppermost rung of the social ladder was pretty much carved in stone. Unbeknownst to me, that stone was as brittle and insubstantial as a scrap of shale.

The next two and a half years of high school saw me growing a lot closer with the new friends I had made as a freshman. There were four other guys I designated my "best friends" along with Adam. But as the years went on, there was a gradual shift in the group dynamics. When Adam's family life, appearance, and state of mind took a turn for the worse, his standing and influence within the circle ebbed, while my own flourished. But even as our calls to Adam's house were growing less frequent, we all still hung out together as if nothing had changed. By the time senior year rolled along it seemed like I was the only one out of the "infamous" posse to keep Adam abreast of any social events. Even though no one treated Adam any differently during school hours, I'm sure he could feel the tension.

My Friend Becomes an Outcast

The truth is that my friends were now trying to distance themselves from a person who they thought was becoming too boring and too complex for the high school social scene. I tried not to partake in my friends' occasional snubs toward Adam, attempting to convince myself that he was still one of my best friends. But the reality was that I'd begun to feel the same way they did. I like to think these emotions toward Adam took root in me because of how impressionable I was in high school, not because I was truly starting to dislike him. The reason I prefer to chalk it up to a weakness in an as-yet-unformed character rather than to a malevolent nature stems from one, isolated incident, an incident that taught me the meaning of the word "cruelty."

At my school, like at most, the senior prom was considered the event of a lifetime. Everything that surrounded this occasion was taken very seriously, especially the assignment of prom limos. The limo you take to the prom is the last public statement of exactly who your friends were during high school. That's why when my friends decided to exclude Adam from our limo I knew there was going to be a problem. I had to make a choice, either to go with them or with Adam. I resolved not to go with Adam and take the limo my other friends had rented. This was easy to rationalize, since I had been spending more time with them and felt closer to them than to Adam. Even though I would be hurting Adam's feelings, I told myself he'd get over it and tried not to think about it.

Unfortunately, the story didn't end there. My popular friends wanted to go one step further. They wanted to break all ties with Adam. They felt he was bringing them down and did not want to be associated with him any longer. Afraid of risking my own reputation, I remained silent when my friends bad-mouthed Adam behind his back. When my friends confronted Adam and told him that we didn't want to be friends with him anymore, I again remained silent. I remained silent while they pointed out all his inadequacies, while they told him he wasn't fun anymore, while they said he should stop coming up to us in school. And when he eventually cried, I still remained silent. That night was the most horrible night of my life.

My Silence Was Cowardly

Saying nothing was just about the worst thing I could have done. I wanted to defend Adam. I wanted to tell my friends that they had no right to hurt another human being like that, much less a former friend. But I couldn't. I didn't have the strength. After the confrontation, I could barely stand to look at myself in the mirror. I knew what I'd done, and telling myself that it wasn't my fault was of no help to my guilty conscience.

During the prom, everyone was drinking, dancing, and partying. But all I could think about was that Adam wasn't with us. This was supposed to be the best night of my life, but I didn't enjoy it. I ran into Adam at the prom. He looked at me, and we both knew what was on each other's mind. But this time it was I who would cry. Not wanting anyone to see how upset I was, I escaped to the bathroom. The tears made my face red and blotchy, but my friends never knew the real reason I looked so bad that night. They laughed at me, saying that I had drunk too much. And just as I was about to laugh along with them, I realized that I didn't have to. High school was over, and so were most of my so-called "friendships."

We Had a "Popularity Plan"

Aislinn Hunter

In this selection, Aislinn Hunter writes about the high school clique she belonged to. Always somewhat on the periphery, she tried incredibly hard to be like the other girls and allowed herself to be ignored, used, and marginalized by the leaders of the group. She explains that she simply wanted to be liked.

I'm often amazed that I survived high school. Given how awful it was, how insecure I was, it's a miracle I came out of it liking myself at all. If through some weird wormhole or freak form of time travel I could zip back and meet the person I was then, maybe in the hallway by my grade ten locker, I don't know if I'd hug her or hit her. I'd probably try to shake some sense into her, tell her about the things that really matter. There is life after high school, I'd say. Or maybe I'd do what I did best back then: avoid confrontation, avert my eyes, and keep walking.

In Grade 9 Our Clique Is Formed

How it looked to everyone else. A crowd of girls, in the requisite kilts and blouses, are walking from one side of our high school campus to the other. They move in that golden kind of slow motion reserved for girl-gets-guy teen movies: kilts swish, hair is flipped casually over shoulders, textbooks are held in the crooks of their arms. When they reach the street, cars stop to let them pass. One of the girls, Kate, lowers her chin and winks at the male driver who's waving her across. She's like something out of a skin-care commercial—big smile, white teeth, perfect complexion, blonde highlights in light-brown hair. Over by the parking lot a few grade twelve basketball all-

Aislinn Hunter, *You Be Me: Friendship in the Lives of Teen Girls*, Toronto: Annick Press, 2002. Copyright © 2002 Aislinn Hunter. All rights reserved. Reproduced by permission.

stars are watching the girls. They're leaning against a sporty green Alfa Romeo, and when they see the girls looking, they wave. Debbie, a girl with dark hair in long braids, rolls her eyes, waves back. Then the girls carry on. All eight of them, the sun shining down on them as they enter the doors of St. Anne's Secondary, heading in for class.

How it looked to me. Kate is bulldozing her way across campus with all of us in tow. I'm trying to keep up. It's spring, and the gang has dressed for it—Esprit blouses tucked into kilts, a short-sleeved Guess button-down on Caroline, Debbie in a crew-neck Ralph Lauren. The kilt and cardigan are part of the mandatory uniform, but we can wear whatever kind of white top we want. I hold my books in front of me like a shield. Under my cardigan I'm wearing a big Hanes T-shirt I took out of my brother's closet. It hangs down over the pleats of my kilt, making me look as large as a semi. I'm obviously "the fat one." And my hair is too short to flip. Walking en masse, we head across the road. Kate is talking about next week's party at Caroline and Christy's house. Who to invite, who to avoid. I listen in.

Over by the parking lot, some of the grade twelve guys wave in our direction. They're always hanging around our lockers and inviting us to after-game parties, even though we're only in grade nine. Next year all the girls I'm walking with will go to the prom, although we'll still be two years away from being seniors. Not me, though. I won't get asked. That kind of thing is a given.

Friends. Kate, Debbie, Danielle, Tracy, Caroline and Christy (the twins), Colette, and me. We are a clique. This is what our principal, Mr. Stanley, calls tight-knit, exclusive groups of friends. He uses the word one day at the podium during an assembly. He's trying in his naive way to address issues that make life difficult in what he calls "the teen years." He has a saying: "Name it. Claim it. Tame it." Whatever your problem is—drugs, alcohol, bullying, isolation—those are the steps to resolve it, a kind of cure-all.

Part of being cool in high school is pretending that *nothing* is cool. That's what Danielle told me. So, when the principal tries to reach out to students with his "I've been there" advice, you're supposed to sit in the bleachers and look at him like he's an idiot. And when slackers stand up in class and mock the principal's three-step program, you look at them like they're idiots, too. Apparently, it gets easier as you go along.

We sit in the stands, ignore the principal, and pass notes or scan the crowd for grade twelve boys. Later we'll meet up in the cafeteria and talk some more about Caroline and Christy's party. I'll go because I'm part of the clique. Because even though I don't really like most of these girls, they are my friends.

Finding the Other Cool Girls

Everyone loves Dani. She's smart and stylish, way ahead of her years. In grade seven when the rest of us were still reading Judy Blume, she was buying *Vogue* and *Cosmopolitan*, and on the nights her dad stayed at his girlfriend's, she made her own dinner and stayed home alone. Most of the kids from our grade school were planning to attend one of the public high schools nearby, but Dani and I knew we'd be going to St. Anne's. It was the only private school in our district. One day in class, just before graduation, Dani handed me a note. It said, "It's time to work on our popularity plan for high school."

I spend the first day of high school worrying about how I look. We're in dress code that day, so no jeans, cords, or T-shirts; no logos; and nothing ripped. I've borrowed these weird green-and-yellow elf boots my older sister bought in Sweden. I'm wearing them with a black skirt and an ugly yellow blouse my sister said would make me look thin. Danielle is looking elegant in a navy cotton blouse and tailored gray dress pants. I chew gum and stare down at my boots throughout the opening assembly. Dani surveys the crowd, picking out the coolest-looking grade nine girls. Within an hour we've latched on to Kate and Debbie.

Over the next few weeks a clique starts to form, and Dani is welcomed in. These girls are pretty, rich, athletic. They do well in school, and they care a lot about clothes. Generally, they are unself-conscious. I'm not any of those things. I'm the opposite: artsy, funny, pretty only in a she-has-a-nice-face sort of way, and completely obsessed with what people think of me. But Dani throws me a life ring. Just as the clique is about to set sail, she pulls me aboard. The group starts hanging out, and Dani makes sure I'm always there.

Caroline and Christy's party is at their house on Riverside Drive. The twins' father is an architect, and they live in a colossal three-story mansion with huge front doors and a backyard view over the pool to the river. There are intercoms in most of the rooms so that Caroline and Christy's mother doesn't have to go up two flights of stairs to announce that dinner is ready. Parties are generally a civilized thing in our clique; the girls sit around eating chips and drinking fruit-flavored coolers, talking about guys or clothes or gossiping about school. This is the worst kind of room to be stuck in when you feel like you don't belong. Packed house parties with loud music and nameless faces offer lots of distractions, but sitting in a living room with seven other people means I'm expected to contribute to the conversation. We're talking about a movie we saw last week at the mall. I say, "That actress is so cool," but Kate gives me a dirty look, repeats "cool" as if it's a crime to say the word. In the silence that follows, I head to the fridge on the pretext of getting another drink. No one says anything as I walk by. No one ever contradicts Kate. In true clique fashion they smile at her, at each other, and then the conversation carries on.

In Grade 10 the Clique Overwhelms Me

How it looked to everyone else. The sun is shining, and a group of pretty girls are eating their lunches on the lawn of St. Anne's south campus. Stan's Chip Van is set up in the parking lot nearby, but the girls are eating yogurt and fruit or sandwiches with alfalfa sprouts sticking out between the crusts. Everyone is dieting, because it's almost summer. From a distance, the kilts spread out on the grass look like the petals of a giant plaid flower. Silvio, a good-looking senior, comes over and plops down next to Tracy. They're going out. A few of Silvio's friends stop to talk to him for a minute, surveying the girls before high-fiving Silvio and moving on. Kate and Colette watch them go, leaning back on their elbows. Someone is playing a car stereo, and the music comes out through the car's open windows. Silvio taps his fingers on Tracy's leg in time with the drumbeat. Everyone's in a good mood because there are only two weeks left before summer vacation.

How it looked to me. The other girls are so relaxed. I can't even find a comfortable way to sit. I'm trying, by shifting my position again and again, to relay some kind of natural serenity. But no matter what I do, I end up feeling fat and tense. Part of the problem is that it's 85° out, and I'm still wearing my cardigan. The other girls are stripped down to their short-sleeved blouses. The sun is making Kate's freckles come out, and Colette already has a tan. Debbie and the twins look like they've been to Hawaii. I'm about as tanned as my white deck shoes. The greasy paper cup that held my French-fry lunch is crumpled on my lap. Later, when everyone heads off to class, I'll go to the girls' washroom and stick my finger down my throat. As usual, I'll try four or five times to barf, but when it doesn't work I'll give up and walk to class. It's like an after-school special on TV, except for this: most of the TV characters with an eating disorder know they have one, and it's a very big deal. It isn't a big deal to me. I don't think about it at all until I find myself stuffing food down my throat and then trying to throw it back up again. The whole thing seems routine by now, as normal as brushing my hair, as putting on lipstick.

Friends. Taken as a group, the clique overwhelms me. I consider Tracy, Colette, and Dani genuine friends. Still, there's an unspoken rule that says we must all hang out together, checking out guys or shopping or meeting up to trade clothes. But Kate can't stand me, it's a fact. And I don't really get along with Debbie or the twins either. One afternoon at Kate's house, there's a serious clothes exchange under way. As usual I'm there but sitting out, because everyone is a size eight and I'm a size twelve. This time, though, up for offer in the show-and-swap is an Esprit top of Kate's that I love, blue and green and blousy. I hate Kate. I think she's mean and shallow. But I ask if I can try it on anyway. The top fits, barely. I get to borrow it for two weeks, the standard trading time, and I wear it almost constantly when I'm not in my school uniform. It's like some strange flag of acceptance.

Everyone in the clique except me goes out on dates. There are two pools of guys the girls draw from: the seniors and the grade ten cool guys. Tracy is dating Silvio, Dani is dating Teddy, Christy is dating Rob. Debbie is going out with the basketball team's all-star. Sometimes the relationships last and sometimes they don't. Either way, there is a steady stream of guys hanging around us at lunch and after class. I have two crushes: one on Pete, a senior who is really nice to me, and one on Corey, a guy in our grade who hangs around with the cool guys. My most secret desire is that one of them will notice me, look at me like they're seeing me for the first time. Like in the movies, I'll be standing around with my friends in the school hallway, then the crowd will part and Pete or Corey will walk over and say "Hey." Just like that: "Hey." Then the two of us will walk slowly down the hall together and out the front doors.

In Grade 11 I Start to Question My Friendships

How it looked to everyone else. A bunch of senior guys are standing by my locker. I share the locker with Colette, and she's dating Jim, who's a star player on the football team. There are even "in" places to have a locker. Ours is on the corner of the main and secondary hallways, where there's lots of traffic. Pete opens his locker, which is next to ours, and finds a huge bra hanging on the hook inside. Colette and I start laughing. We snuck it in there after spying on Pete's lock combination. Jim takes the bra and wraps it around his head, then starts dancing around, two polyester double-D cups hanging down over his ears. Students walk by gaping. We're still laughing when the bell goes.

How it looked to me. I'm walking across campus bundled in my new purple winter coat, which I think is pretty stylish. Colette and I part just outside the doors of the south campus building, because she has English this period and I have Math in the farthest portable. Randy Arsenault, one of the cool grade eleven guys, is hanging around outside having a smoke. He waves as I go by. Then he calls out "Nice coat, Grimace!" before turning back to his friends. He thinks it's hysterical; they all do. I smirk in their general direction and keep walking. No one ever says anything like that when the rest of the girls are around.

Friends. At home, my mother says things like "Don't let people use you" and "Is she really that good a friend?" She sees the warning signs. I shrug and say, "Oh, Kate's cool" or "Dani's going to be there," and that seems to appease her. My mom sees me less often now that I'm sixteen and have a car. It's just a beat-up Honda, but I'm the only one in the clique with wheels. I'm always heading out the door to drive the girls somewhere. I bend over backwards for Kate and Debbie and the twins, no matter what they need. My mom says, "Honey, I'm worried they're taking advantage of you."

Some mornings, when I'm feeling down, I stop at the 7-Eleven to buy chocolate milk, Twinkies, and chips. I down them a block from school, then try to throw them up when I get to the girls' washroom. Even though I've taken to carrying a spoon in my purse, using the handle to reach as far back into my throat as it will go, I usually can't quite manage to get rid of everything.

Sometime around October, Tracy starts going out with Mike, another guy from the football team. He's totally hot. I know him because I've been volunteering as the statistician for the senior boys' football team. I do this with Marianne, who's a satellite member of the clique. It's fun to feel important, to sit on the bench keeping track of the plays and tackles. One night after winning a game against our big rivals, there's a party at the quarterback's house. Marianne and I get to go along, even though the players' girlfriends aren't invited. After the party, Mike and I end up getting a ride from this guy Jeff, who like us lives a fair distance outside the city. We're pretty drunk, so we sit in the back and call Jeff "Jeeves," pretending he's our chauffeur. Halfway home, Mike and I start making out. Things get hot and heavy, and eventually Jeff pulls over onto a dirt road and tells us he's getting out of the car "so you two can be alone." When he opens the car door and the interior light comes on, Mike and I snap out of it. Jeff gets back into the driver's seat and takes us home. The next day Tracy sits with me in Science class like she always does, passing me notes over the lab counter. She's always telling me how funny I am and trying to bolster my self-esteem. She defends me in front of Kate, too. Tracy never finds out what happened in the car, but that whole week I wallow in guilt. I can't even look at Mike or Jeff when I pass them in the hall.

In Grade 12 I Find Myself

How it looked to everyone else. The cafeteria is jam-packed, and the noise level is unbelievable. A group of guys standing by the far wall talk about their first-semester finals, plan a big party for the week after the last exam. This year there's been a fair bit of gossip about the new transfer students and the exchange student from Sweden, which is probably the price you pay for being new. Inge, her über-blonde hair in ringlets, sits by the cafeteria entrance. As usual, she's getting a lot of attention. The eight of us are sitting by the back doors, at the same table we always sit at. Kate and Dani, kilts fanned out over the bench, flip through a magazine. Colette and Tracy talk about the prom. People are already pairing up for it. No one is discussing academics. The big question is who, from our clique, will be prom queen. Last year it was Amy Paulin, one of the most popular girls in the class above ours. This year at a school assembly she gave a speech about her anorexia. She said she had almost died in the hospital the previous summer. This is the first time eating disorders have been addressed in school. Still, people treat it like gossip. "Name it, claim it, tame it," Principal Stanley said after Amy walked off the stage. We scuffed our shoes on the bleachers, rolled our eyes, and cracked our bubble gum.

How it looked to me. Maneuvering. How to get from the cafeteria table, where prom dates and dresses are the hot topic, to the bathroom without creating a fuss. I wrap up what's left of my sub and shove it into my lunch bag. Lifting my leg over the bench, I lose my balance and bump Tracy with my arm. "Be right back," I announce. No one says anything. They're listening to Kate, who's telling everyone strapless dresses are out, cleavage is in. Kate and Dani are dating two new guys, Richard and Wayne. They're transfer students from a tough city school, definitely not *GQ* but cool and edgy enough to seem like good catches. I'm hoping to go to the prom with Corey. It's a matter of math. There are eight guys and eight girls in the two popular cliques. Since he isn't seeing anyone, I sort of assume we'll go together, to keep the groups intact. But I'm wrong. Corey tells me at one of the basketball games that he's taking Rachel Manning, a girl from my Music class. I'm stumped. I don't get it. I spend the whole of Science class writing furtive notes to Tracy. "She's nobody!" I scribble. "She isn't even pretty."

Friends. Dani has decided to bring this girl Tamara into our clique. Like Wayne and Richard, Tamara is a transfer student from another school. Dani starts inviting Tamara to all the group functions even though Kate and the twins don't seem to care for her. What amazes me is that Tamara doesn't put up with Kate's crap. An unofficial rift develops in the group's gatherings: Tamara and me are on one side; Dani, Tracy, Debbie, and Colette are somewhere in the middle. Kate and the twins are on the other side. Dani, as usual, is the glue that holds us all together.

Everything Changes Before Prom

Two months before the prom, things between Kate and Wayne go sour. That means things with Richard and Dani go downhill, too. The four of them hung around together all the time. A final, huge argument between Kate and Wayne takes place by the football field. Wayne points at Kate a lot, jabs at her shoulder with his finger while a group of us watch from a distance. Kate never tells us what happened.

Wayne sits two rows away from me in English class. We've always said hi before, gone to the same parties, but I don't really know him. After the breakup he nods my way every now and again. Sometimes he passes me notes, small folded-up pieces of paper with "How's it going?" scrawled in bad handwriting. I decide he's testing the waters to see how much his breakup with Kate has affected his relationship with everyone else in the clique. I write him back.

About a week after the football field ruckus, during a class on Steinbeck, Wayne sends me a note that says, "They're so shallow. Why do you hang around with them, anyway? You can do better." I don't know what to reply. I mean, these are my friends.

Name it. Claim it. Tame it.

I want to be liked. It's that simple.

The end of the year is just around the corner, and I'm close to failing Economics and History. If I fail, I won't get my grade twelve diploma. Either way, I'm glad it's almost over. I don't think I can put up with even one more month of high school. Wayne and I have been spending lots of time together, not just at school but at parties and at my house. Kate's practically stopped speaking to me. Wayne's not at all like I thought he would be. He doesn't give a shit about who's in and who isn't. He's also kind of a loner. He's the first guy I've met I really feel I can be friends with.

During the last month of school, I see a lot of Tamara. Like Wayne, she doesn't take crap from anyone. She even looks tough: fiery red hair, dark freckles, eyes that narrow easily into slits. She has a response for everything. Before school ends, I get a part-time job at a restaurant near the university. It's a great job and a cool hangout. Moving away from the clique is easier than I thought it would be, It's liberating.

I do go to the prom. Colette is named prom queen, and half the clique are the official prom princesses. Tamara and I go together, because we don't want to miss out. We take along my older sister's friend Dave, who works at the restaurant with me. We thought it would be fun to show up with a total stranger who's five years older. Dave is a graduate of St. Anne's too, so for him it's a blast from the past.

The dress I wear looks hideous. Midway through the evening Tamara, who's really drunk, starts dancing on a large speaker beside the stage. I get out my Polaroid camera and take a photo of her. She comes down off the speaker to cheers and applause.

The three of us head to a nearby hotel room for the after-prom party. We stay for a few drinks, then Dave drives us home. At my house I wave him off, watch his car reverse down the driveway and swing out onto the road. It's late, about three in the morning. Everything is dark and still. I take the camera from my bag and hold it out at arm's length in front of me. I smile into the lens, push the shutter button. The flash goes off. The picture slides out. I stand under the porch light, waiting to see how it will turn out.

CHAPTER 3

| Finding Personal Identity

Finding My Own Crowd

Jodee Blanco

Jodee Blanco is a public relations specialist in the book publishing and entertainment industries. Before she entered into a highly successful career, she spent years battling degradation at school. When she became an adolescent and developed a problem which made her breasts grow unevenly, she was mocked even more. Eventually, as she relates in this excerpt from her memoirs, she finds an interesting group of friends who help her feel accepted.

Since the incident after gym [when my classmates became aware of my misshapen breasts, they] have decided they won't allow a "freak" like me to eat in their lunchroom. When they see me at the soda machines, they threaten to beat me. They have made me so scared that I start stuffing my bookbag with breakfast bars and protein snacks each morning before school. Then, at lunchtime, I sneak into the girls' bathroom, sit on the sink, and wolf them down. I have nowhere else to go. Students aren't allowed to leave the school grounds for lunch and eating isn't permitted in class.

One afternoon, Ms. Linstrom, the school librarian and a sweet older woman, finds me in the lavatory. She wraps her arms around me. She gives me a pass for the rest of the semester so that I can have my lunch in the library with her. I confide in Ms. Linstrom the agony I'm going through. She tells me that my classmates are tough on me not because they hate me, but because they don't understand me. "One day your life will change and you'll have so many friends . . . people with whom you have something in common," she says reassuringly.

In the Library I Find Refuge

I love spending time in the library with Ms. Linstrom. It's safe; no one can hurt me there. I read biographies about famous living people and vow that one day I will be part of their lives. Ms. Linstrom also encourages me to write and has entered me in a poetry competition. If I win, I will be given a scholarship to a two-week summer writing and acting workshop at Eastern Illinois University. I cross my fingers.

I manage to keep my spirits up by concentrating on [my trip to the Greek island of] Santorini. Yorgos and his friends send me letters every week and Niko and I talk on the phone often. I'm proud of myself for learning such a difficult language. My dad's proud of me too—he promises that if I keep my grades up and continue progressing with my second language, he'll let me use one of his company cars.

In the interim, I still ride the bus to and from school. The kids are relentless in making fun of my deformity, which is still hot gossip. Every day is a new adventure in humiliation. Almost every afternoon, it's the same routine. I get off the bus, someone knocks me down, grabs my books, and throws them into the middle of the street. I watch while cars run over my books and papers. When there's a break in traffic, I rush out and quickly gather the scattered remnants. One day, I lose my temper. As two of the kids begin shoving and pushing me, I scream "Screw you!" as loudly as I can. They only laugh. The next thing I know, they are grabbing my shoulders and pretending they're going to push me into the street. They are stronger than they think—they push me into traffic and two cars came to a screeching halt just feet away. I never take the bus again. My grandfather, who saw what happened from the window, begins driving me to school every morning and picking me up each afternoon. Though the circumstances that force us together are unfortunate, the time I spend with him is priceless.

A Not-So-Merry Christmas

With each passing day, I can feel my resolve slipping away. Christmas has me down and out. Mom senses something, but isn't pushing me to open up. I guess she figures I'll talk about it when I'm ready. Instead, she busies herself preparing for Christmas. My parents love the holidays. The interior of our home looks like the display window at Marshall Field's. Each member of our family has an assignment in the decorating process. Mom and dad are in charge of the tree; grandmother is responsible for wrapping garland and strings of lights around all the picture frames, mirrors, and railings in the house; and my grandfather and I do the elves, my favorite part.

Years ago, the company that makes Joy dishwashing liquid did a special holiday promotion. For every bottle you purchased, you received a felt Christmas elf. My mom fell in love with these little, smiling figurines, and she must have collected fifty. Grandfather and I spent hours finding just the right places to put them. It was like a treasure hunt. We perched them on lampshades and nestled them among the leaves of my mom's indoor plants. We even had them peeking out of the medicine cabinets in the bathrooms.

Despite all the extravagant decorations, Christmas is subdued. My grandparents, aunts, mom, dad, and I have a traditional ham dinner and exchange gifts. Though I make a grand show of it for my family, ripping the wrapping paper off my presents and diving into the boxes, my mind is somewhere else. I envision Jacklyn and her boyfriend nuzzling each other by a cozy fire; Tyler and his girl drinking eggnog with their friends. I fight back tears.

"Jodee, why don't you sing us a Christmas carol?" dad suggests.

The last thing I want to do is burst into song. But I love my dad and want to make him happy. I belt out "O Holy Night." Everyone claps as I smile and sit down. Shu Shu, our poodle, jumps into my lap, wagging her tail so furiously that it creates a breeze. As I pet her fluffy black ears, I try to imagine what Christmas will be like for me a decade from now. Will I have a career? Will I be married? Will my family be okay? I wish the universe would rush the passage of time so that years would turn into months, and days would become hours. I realize it's probably a sin to think like this, but I want my teen years to finish. If they don't end soon, I fear they may finish *me*.

By the time school reconvenes after Christmas break, I am out of optimism. The loneliness is unbearable. My parents aren't stupid—they see my disposition deteriorating. I finally decide to tell them what's been happening these last few months.

"Are you sure you won't consider transferring to another high school?" dad asks. "At least think about it for next year."

"Okay, daddy. I will."

A New Friend Appears

The next few weeks move at a snail's pace. The teasing at school has grown so intense that I'm exhausted by the end of each day. I still have one more year before I can have plastic surgery to fix my breasts. The surgeons keep telling us the same thing: "Not until she's at least seventeen." My chest hurts so much I can't sleep on my stomach. My doctor has offered to prescribe painkillers, but I don't want any part of them. The last time a specialist gave me pills, I practically turned into a zombie. I'd rather hurt than be spaced out.

Mom continues to be encouraging. Though I usually find her optimism irritating, today it proves prophetic. As I'm walking out of gym, one of the girls from my English class stops me in the hall. Tall with short red hair and a tomboyish exterior, Annie is considered a loner. Because she is always dressed in tight jeans and a black leather jacket, no one ever messes with her. Even Sharon and her crowd are intimidated by Annie's toughness. I can't imagine what she wants to talk to me about.

"Hey, Jodee, I'm having a couple of friends over Friday night, and I was wondering if you wanted to join us," Annie says.

"Are you serious?" I ask, dumbstruck.

"Yeah, why wouldn't I be?" she answers.

"It's just that the few times I've been invited to anything, it's always turned out to be a mean joke," I reply.

"I think it's really cool how you hold your head up despite how bad everyone treats you. You've got a lot of guts. You should forget about these assholes at Samuels and get to know my friends. They'd like you."

"Okay. For sure, I'll come," I respond. We exchange phone numbers and addresses. Friday after school, I can barely contain my excitement. "Mom, what should I wear tonight?" I ask.

"Honey, put on whatever makes you feel the prettiest," my mom advises.

Preparing for the Unknown

I choose an off-white silk blouse and my lavender Gloria Vanderbilt jeans. I dab a tiny bit of lilac perfume on my wrists. "It's getting late," mom says. "Coming," I respond. Within minutes, we are on our way to Annie's. Her parents have offered to let me spend the night. As we pull into her driveway, Annie and her mom come out to greet us.

"Mrs. Blanco, it's nice to meet you," Annie says. "This is my mom, Virginia." It's hard for me to believe this sweet, caring girl who's treating my mom with such respect is the same person feared by half of Samuels.

"It's so good to meet you both," mom responds. "Jodee has really been looking forward to this evening."

"Annie, too," Virginia says. "Oh, to be that age again."

They chat for a few moments, then my mom leaves.

"Your mom's really cool," Annie remarks as we go into the house.

"Thanks," I reply.

"We'll hang out downstairs," Annie says. "My friends should be here soon."

I follow Annie down a short flight of steps to a large rec room. At the far end is a small round table with platters of hot and cold food and a cooler with cans of soda on ice.

"Who do you want to listen to?" she asks, turning on the stereo. "I've got Rush, Journey, Led Zeppelin . . ."

"Journey," I reply. The rich voice of lead singer Steve Perry fills the room.

"I love this song," Annie comments.

"Yeah, me too," I agree. "Can I ask you something?"

"Sure, shoot."

"You pretend to be so tough at school. But you're really not like that at all. Why the act?"

"Don't be fooled. I'm no angel. I like it that the 'popular' girls are afraid of me. I used to be made fun of, same as you," Annie recalls. "Then I got smart. I figured if I looked tough, I'd be left alone. I was right. I don't think a person needs to be mean to be feared. The girls at school see the chain hanging from my belt buckle and my tattoos, and they're scared to death, but I've never teased a single person at Samuels. I wouldn't do it because I know what that feels like and it's the worst feeling on earth."

A Clique of My Own

As we're talking, two young men arrive who appear to be about nineteen or twenty years old. Annie makes the introductions. "Jodee, this is Bill and Dino. Guys, meet Jodee."

Bill is tall and gangly. His blond hair is cut close to his head. Clad in ripped faded jeans, a Ted Nugent T-shirt, and black army boots, he reminds me of a character out of a

1960s biker movie. He can't stand still—he's constantly shifting his weight from one foot to the other.

Heavyset with a kind smile and curly black hair, Dino looks like Winnie the Pooh in Harley Davidson garb. His calm demeanor is a stark contrast to Bill's frenetic energy.

They both say, "Hello."

"Want a cigarette?" Bill asks, pulling a pack of Marlboros out of his pocket and offering one to me.

"No, thanks," I respond.

"You don't smoke. That's cool. I wish I could quit," he says, turning and walking toward the buffet table.

"He seems like a really nice guy," I remark.

"He gets into trouble sometimes," Annie says. "But he's such a good person. He's always there when I need him."

"Does he live at home?"

"No, that's the problem," Dino says. "His parents are super-strict. It doesn't help that he's adopted, either. He got so tired of them constantly trying to control him that he finally just packed up and left."

"God, that's awful."

"Yeah," Dino agrees. "I feel bad for him. He lives in this tiny studio apartment and he's always struggling to make his rent."

"What does he do?"

"Whatever he can. Odd jobs. He sells a little weed here and there. Don't say anything to my mom. She likes Bill but she worries he's a 'bad influence' on me. She'd flip out if she knew about the pot thing."

"Everybody, look who's here," Bill shouts.

"Didn't anyone ever tell you not to talk with your mouth full?" says the handsome guy coming down the stairs.

"Who's that?" I ask.

"My brother, David," Annie replies, watching me scope him out. "Boy, are you barking up the wrong tree," she says.

"What do you mean?" I ask.

"What she means is that I'm gay," David answers.

"You're kidding!"

"Nope, but if I were straight, I'd be after you in a flash," he says, walking toward us.

"Thanks," I reply, smiling.

The rest of the evening, the five of us talk. We discuss everything from drugs, dating, and sex to movies and music. We share stories about our past, and the rejection we've suffered. I am beginning to see that the *cool crowd* at Samuels plays in a very small sandbox. Annie's friends operate on a much larger playing field. They're out in the world in a way that most high school kids aren't. Something about how they carry themselves and the way they talk makes me think of the tragic heroes of ancient Greek literature. They have freedom and mobility. They're doing things on their own, even if they aren't things that society approves of. They're a struggling version of the people who make a difference in the world—the artists, the musicians, and the actors. I discover that I share a sensibility with them.

These Friendships Deepen

These older misfits give me a social circle. They tell me that the "cool" kids are just conventional people doing dumb things. I still have to contend with them because they're in school, but these new older friends convince me that I no longer need to worry about emulating my popular classmates. They offer relief because they absolve me of being an accessory in my own punishment.

We are inseparable the rest of the semester. They help me out of my self-loathing and I help them get their lives back on track. A lot of kids like this are defiant because they think nobody cares. I show them that somebody *does* care about them. My dad helps Bill find steady work, and my grandfather lets Dino sleep over when things get too hot at home. My parents open their arms to them, inviting them on weekend trips and including them at family gatherings. First to my amazement and then to my delight, my family find Bill and Dino as interesting and amusing as I do.

I have to hand it to my mom. She always tells me that when God closes one door, he opens another. As I sit curled up in the comfortable overstuffed chair in the family room talking to Annie on the phone, I realize that she's right.

"Annie, wait a minute, someone's calling on the other line. Hello?"

"Jodee, it's Ms. Linstrom."

"Hi!"

"I've got some wonderful news. I just received a letter from Eastern Illinois University. The judges were very impressed by your poetry. You won the scholarship for the summer writing workshop!"

"Oh, Ms. Linstrom, I'm so excited!"

"Come by my office on Monday and we'll fill out the paperwork."

"Thanks. See you then. Bye, Ms. Linstrom."

I click back to the other line.

"Annie, you'll never guess what happened!"

Friends of All Races

Cassandra Thadal

Cliques can be created for a variety of reasons. One notable reason is to maintain racial or ethnic groups. In this situation, there is comfort in being with people who understand you, share your culture, and often speak your own language. Many immigrants find that hanging out with others from their country of origin makes them feel less homesick and frightened. But, like any clique, racial and ethnic groups can be very tight and exclusive, closing others out. When she was fifteen, Cassandra Thadal decided that she was practicing a form of racism by limiting her friendships to the group of Haitian girls at her school, and in this essay Thadal describes this realization.

Here's a scene from a typical day in my high school classroom: students from various countries, such as Mexico, Poland, Bangladesh, Yemen, and the Dominican Republic, are talking and laughing as they work together and help each other.

The teacher yells, "Why am I hearing you talking? Shouldn't you be working?"

"We work and talk at the same time," we answer.

Division at Lunchtime

When the clock marks lunchtime, we rush out of our classroom and head for the cafeteria. But by the time we reach our destination, the kids who mixed happily in the classroom have left that spirit of unity behind.

At most of the tables in the cafeteria, you see faces of the same color. The students enjoy this time with their own folks.

The kids say they do this because it's just more comfortable. So whoever arrives in the cafeteria first gets her food and spots some seats, then saves a place for others of her same race or ethnic group.

After lunch, they leave together and spend the rest of the period in the hallways, or outside if it's not cold. A group of Polish kids settles on the floor near the main office, chatting and gossiping. Sometimes other Polish kids play checkers or dice nearby.

Some of the Dominicans sit in the hallway a few feet from the Polish kids. Most of the time they talk loudly and sing in Spanish or dance. A little further along, some kids from Ecuador or Peru hang out. The Bengalis gather in one classroom, listening to Bengali music.

The Haitian girls—the group I am part of—hang out next to our counselor's office, while the Haitian boys assemble on the stairs.

The students are allowed to roam around freely like this because my school is very small and generally there's harmony. People may have their personal disagreements, but groups rarely fight. That doesn't mean that everybody's friends, though—they aren't.

Of course, some teens do befriend people from different races. One Polish girl often hangs with a Filipina girl, and there are two black guys, one from France, the other from Africa, who are friends with a kid from Mexico.

A Variety of Friends

I am also someone who doesn't stick only to her own race—although this wasn't always the case. When I first arrived here I had never spent any time with white people.

I lived in Haiti until I was 14. When I saw white people in Haiti, I hated them because I knew that whites had enslaved and mistreated blacks. I didn't know any whites who considered blacks their equals.

Also, some Haitians said, "Oh, the whites are so smart!" whenever they saw great things like computers or cars, as if no black person could invent things, and I hated that.

When I moved to the United States, I began to experience being around people of other races. I sat in a classroom and saw all different kinds of people. I wanted to talk to them—except the whites. My friends were Chinese, Honduran, and Haitian.

But when I saw the white kids, I said to myself, "I am not going to talk to these people." I assumed they were saying the same thing because I'm black. But gradually my attitude changed.

The white kids at school treated me nicely, and I saw that many blacks were doing great at my school. It seemed like in the United States, whether you were black or white, you could do great things. In class I learned that we all had things in common and I began to feel comfortable. My friends and I often discussed racism. We thought that teenagers should mix. Our culture and skin color differed, but we ignored our differences in the classroom and got along very well.

Friends of One Race

So it surprised me that when I returned to school last fall, I stopped mingling with other races and stayed with two Haitian girls. It didn't happen that way because I was being a racist, or at least I didn't think so.

It was because my Honduran friend, Daysa, was not yet back from vacation, and most of my old Chinese friends were in other classes. So every day during lunch, I started sitting with the Haitian girls.

After Daysa came back, I still spent most of my time with the Haitians. Daysa spoke with her friends in Spanish and I spoke Haitian Creole with my friends. I didn't see any problem with this until one day I got to the lunchroom before my two Haitian friends.

A friend of mine from the Dominican Republic asked me to sit with her, so I did. When my Haitian friends came, they looked at me strangely, but I didn't react and just said, "Hi." Then I ate my lunch and talked to the Dominican girl.

Later, when my Haitian friends were leaving, they passed and said, "Oh, yeah, Cassandra, you're buying the Spanish face." ("Buying someone's face" is a Haitian expression. It means that you ignore your own race and stay with another one because you think that the other race is superior, even if that race is disrespectful to you.)

I laughed and said, "What do you mean I'm buying the Spanish face? Sitting with someone Spanish has nothing to do with that." Later I talked with one of my friends and told her that what they said wasn't fair and didn't make me happy.

"Okay, girl," she said, and that was it. We were again at peace.

I didn't take these things too seriously. They sounded more like jokes to me. But soon I realized they were not jokes. Later in the year, I became friends with a Russian girl named Natasha. We were in the same group in class and she was very nice to me. We always talked to each other in class and she often called me on the telephone, but we never sat together at lunch.

Making My Own Decisions

One day my Haitian friends were sitting at our table while I was still standing in line. After I got my meal I saw Natasha and she called to me. "Come sit with me!" "Oh . . . I'm sorry. I have to sit with the Haitians or else they will say that I'm buying your face. You know . . ."

"What?" Natasha said, confused. I explained the expression and she said, "Okay, I'll see you later."

I left her by herself and went to my other friends. Because I didn't want my Haitian friends to tease me, I stopped hanging out with people of other races.

Sometimes in the morning I still walked around with one of the Chinese guys who had been my friend since ninth grade. My friends from Haiti never said anything about that, but another Haitian girl told me, "Cassandra, you love the Chinese too much. You're buying their faces."

I laughed and told her she was wrong. Still, I kept my friendship with kids from other races inside the classroom, because I hated what my Haitian friends said whenever I hung out with them at lunch.

The Haitian students mean a lot to me and I always try to get along with them because they're my people. I never told them how much I was bothered by what they said. Then I started to write this story, and I began to think about how we were all acting.

I realized I had become a different person by not mixing with other students when I wanted to. And when I realized that, I decided to change back to who I really am.

Now, in the cafeteria, I sit with Natasha, my Russian friend, along with my Honduran friend, Daysa.

I had stopped mixing with other kids because I was scared of what my friends would think and say. It's good to stay with "your people" sometimes. But, at the same time, if you only stay with your people, you're missing out on a lot of opportunities to make new friends and have new experiences.

We need to break down the walls of language, culture, and skin color if we want racism to stop. We share many common things, but the only way we can find out what they are is if we mix.

Individual Style Is Best

Esther Sooter

In the following selection, sixteen-year-old Esther Sooter recalls a conversation she had with her father when she was in middle school. Focusing on the topic of dress, he impressed upon her that it is more important to be true to who you are than to follow the crowd in order to be popular. Little by little, she recognized the wisdom in this advice.

While in middle school, students seem to have one goal: to be *popular*. More than anything, most of the students fervently hope to not be accused of going against the grain. These young teenagers would much rather conform and be accepted by the "in" crowd than focus on finding their own identity, style or path. Like most thirteen-year-olds, I succumbed to this need to fit in. One afternoon, however, I had a conversation with my father that made me think twice about following the rest of the lemmings over the proverbial cliff.

My dad and I were sitting in the dining area of the local Dairy Queen eating Blizzards on a dreary winter afternoon. We had run the [gamut] of usual conversation topics: school, orchestra, my plans for the weekend. Then, and I'm not quite sure how the discussion began, we started talking about popularity. I told him that I wanted to be popular, or at least accepted favorably by those who were. He looked at me and asked me why I felt that way. I shrugged my shoulders and looked back into my drink. I had never stopped to think about why I felt the need to fit in . . . I simply did. I had been told by my friends that I should want to be popular, and since I had always trusted them, I was inclined to believe them.

A Lesson About Individuality

My father proceeded to tell me a story from his college days. His mother, my grandmother Lorraine, had made him several sweater vests to wear at school. These sweater vests were practical and comfortable, but hardly "in style." Nevertheless, they became a staple of my father's wardrobe. He didn't care that he wasn't sporting the latest fashion. In fact, he didn't care what everyone thought of him, either. I was shocked. What was even more surprising was that after a few weeks, other students at my dad's school began wearing sweater vests. By deviating from the norm, my father had started a trend. What he wore became fashionable because the other students saw the confidence with which he dressed.

This information was a lot for a thirteen-year-old girl to process, especially one who had been carefully taught about what was "cool" and what was most certainly not cool. I found it hard to believe that going against the grain could have benefits for me, so I continued to wear the same clothes, listen to the same music and go to the same places that my peers did. Surely my father was mistaken. This is also, of course, the stage in which children think they know infinitely more than their parents. I had not yet seen the light, and I continued on my quest for popularity. However, our conversation that bleak winter day replayed over and over in my mind.

Appreciating My Father's Wisdom

As the days passed and I mulled it over, I realized that my father's words might have some validity after all. I began to evaluate my wardrobe to find which items I had bought because they were cool and which items I'd bought because I truly liked them. I also looked back at my actions, attempting to determine how many of them I performed to please the crowd and how many of them I performed because I actually enjoyed them. I found myself caring less and less what people thought about me. It was wonderfully liberating.

I have come a long way since middle school. It no longer bothers me that those who still feel compelled to follow the herd do not accept me as one of their own. I do not strive to dress in the latest fashions; if anything, I attempt to create my own. The conversation I had with my father about wearing sweater vests and feeling the need to fit in sparked in me the desire to deviate from the beaten path and form one of my own. I have learned a valuable lesson in the process: Swimming against the current can only make me stronger.

I Chose Academics over Popularity

Jacqueling Nwaiwu

My Sisters' Voices: Teenage Girls of Color Speak Out *is a collection of works written by young women of many racial backgrounds, edited by Iris Jacob. While she was a teenager committed to diversity issues, Jacob started affinity groups for students of color at her high school and became codirector of a youth leadership institute, which addressed topics of oppression, prejudice, and awareness.*

In the following essay, Nigerian American Jacqueling Nwaiwu relates her experiences of watching students at her new high school form into cliques. Ultimately, she chooses to focus on getting a good education even though it degrades her status with the black clique at her school.

As I walked down the crowded halls of Central High on the first day of school, I was overcome with many emotions. I was physically tired because I was not accustomed to waking up so early, and I was also scared and nervous. It was my freshman year, and above all other emotions, nervousness prevailed. I was trembling; my hands were clammy and sweaty. Students were greeting each other. There were clusters of students by lockers chatting away, catching up on all the summer gossip. I continued to walk through the halls observing the madness. Kids were running through the halls playing tag and ramming into each other. Bewildered, I muttered, "So this is high school. It looks more like the circus. So much for thinking that high school is exactly like the preppy, well-mannered students in the weekly TV show *Saved by the Bell*."

I managed to find my homeroom after walking around for fifteen minutes. When I went in, I noticed that over half of the students in my homeroom were students who attended the same junior high as me. I was annoyed with that fact because I wanted to meet new people and make new friends instead of interacting with the same old students from junior high. And with that, I quickly sat down next to a girl with spiky, blue hair, whom I did not know.

Right at that moment, my blond, skinny homeroom teacher, Ms. Larsen, shouted, "Welcome to high school!" She went on, saying, "These next four years will be monumental. These four years will define your character; you will either choose that path of excelling in school or you will decide that socializing with friends is more important. You have two paths to choose from. Today is the first day of school, choose your path wisely."

That statement remained with me for the whole day. I kept thinking to myself, This is the beginning of my high school career, I must do well in school. I must pick the right path.

My Lifelong Goal

Attaining a sound education has been my goal since before I could remember. Every day from the time I was in kindergarten to the present, my parents have always said, in their thick Nigerian accents, "Read hard so that you may be successful." (To my parents, "reading hard" is synonymous with studying rigorously.) I have always endeavored to excel in school and a large portion of my motivation is because of that overused quote. Whenever stress mounts, and I feel that I never want to do another paper or another homework assignment, I always remember what my parents would tell me, "Read hard so that you may be successful."

Schooling is crucial to me. I believe that the better one does in school, the more successful he or she becomes in the real world. I define a successful person as one who is happy, has a great family, and has a great-paying job.

Over the course of the year, every student in my homeroom chose either to take school seriously or to slack off. In homeroom, cliques started to form. The slackers sat on one side of the room, while the studious, grade-conscious students sat on the other side. Students on the slacker side of the room constantly yelled and were rowdy, while the students on the grade-conscious side of the room were busy trying to study or complete homework.

A Startling Confrontation

One day, I came into homeroom and sat in my designated spot: the studious, grade-conscious side of the room. The morning announcements were blaring while I frantically tried to complete my homework. I was completing my math problems when suddenly the bell rang, indicating that it was time for first hour. I ignored it and continued to finish the problems due that hour. Before I knew it, the second bell rang and I was late for math class.

I quickly jammed my books in my bag and ran out of my fourth-floor homeroom. I ran down the hall and up the stairs to the fifth floor. When I got to the fifth floor, I was blocked by a group of African American girls. The five rowdy girls stood in the entrance of the stairwell. I was so agitated. I wanted to push the girls out of my way so I could get to class. But instead, I maneuvered, through the crowd. As I was doing that, one of the girls loudly said, "Who do she think she is anyway, huh?" The group of girls roared with laughter. Another girl said, "Ya'll leave her alone. She trying to get her an edgamacation." And with that, everyone laughed even more. I turned around and looked at them, but said nothing. I simply walked to my math class humiliated.

At that moment, I strongly regretted running down the halls like some geek. I strongly regretted not saying something to them. I strongly regretted having the intense desire to go to my math class and do well in school. It was as if the girls were saying, "Who do she think she is, huh? A black girl trying to be white. An oreo, black on the outside, but white on the inside. Do she think she betta than us? She betta not, 'cause she ain't. School ain't that important for her to be running like that to some class. Some black girls don't know their race. Education ain't all that important. I'd rather clown wit my homies than run to class actin' like I'm white tryin' ta git an education."

Anger and Disappointment Make Things Clear

"Who do she think she is anyway, huh?" I was furious. What exactly did she mean by that? I was only trying to get to class. Excuse me if school means a little more to me than "hangin' out wit da homies." I couldn't believe I gave those girls so much power that they were able to ruin my day.

The next day, I went to homeroom. I mentioned the story to Meg, the girl with the spiky, blue hair. Meg said, "Forget them. School is more important than trying to fit into some popular clique. Look at me. I have blue hair. I try not to fit into groups who don't accept me for me. School is much more important. Don't waste your energy on ignorant people."

Right as she said that, everything was clear. I didn't have to waste my energy on them. I chose schooling over socializing. I chose to study for tests instead of "gossiping over someone's baby's mamma." I selected education over ignorance. I thought to myself, Maybe I am not "ghetto" and maybe I do choose to speak properly. I am not any less black; I am just being me. I preferred work over play, homework instead of fitting into a crowd where I don't belong. I chose schooling.

When looking back at the experience I had with those girls, I thank God every day. That particular experience reaffirmed my goal, which was to attain a sound education. I thank God for giving me the initiative to select the right path, despite all odds.

Being Rejected Strengthened My Spirit

Anonymous

In the following article, the anonymous seventeen-year-old writer emphasizes that the pain of being excluded from a clique can last for years. This essay also shows how the use of e-mail and social networking sites like Facebook and MySpace allows people to make hurtful statements and spread them to huge numbers of people quite easily. In the end, the author finds strength and pride in rejecting her clique's treatment, and she is grateful for the liberating experience.

It is funny how in all the days, weeks, and years in our lifetimes that flee before our eyes, certain memories cannot evade our grasp and continue to live on in our hearts forever. Sometimes it takes the wounded heart years to heal from the inflicted pain, but for some, those scars can leave a permanent mark than can never be erased. I can still feel fierce twinges of pain when I reflect upon my experiences in a friendship that I had in years past. For a while, I tried to forget, but once you have been cut as deeply as I have, the pain cannot just dissipate, for it has been branded into my heart, and will forever continue to leave a lasting impact on my life.

I was just a mere sixth grader, both innocent and naive as I tried to blend in with the rest of the girls in my tight-knit elementary school. At first, I felt content with my group of friends, for although I was not the leader, I was still surrounded by peers, and I was willing to follow along if it guaranteed acceptance. I never anticipated that these girls who I considered friends would make my life a living hell for an entire year. I was very trusting and honestly believed that my friends were good people as well.

The onset of my tarnished friendship started out small, as my group did little things outside of school and failed to invite me along. This caused me some pain, but I tried to have faith that they would include me next time. Soon, it became a regular occurrence, and to make matters worse, I would have to sit in class and listen to them talking about funny stories from the times they had spent together. The only reason I subjected myself to this torment was because when I was with any one of my friends *alone*, she would treat me like a true friend would.

To compensate for my feelings of loneliness and isolation, I tried to include myself into their conversations and act interested in their stories so that I would be included, too. Even when they did include me in their activities, I still felt left out, because they would all stick together and make me feel like an outsider. That year, my sole ambition was to be recognized and accepted by my friends because, more than anything else, I longed for their affection.

The Butt of Their Jokes

Before I knew it, my group of friends started to become more devious and malicious, and I began to realize that their inside jokes were mainly based on poking fun at me. No matter what I did, they always found a way to make me feel embarrassed, whether it was something that I said or even the way I played a sport. The secretive gossip made me feel awful, and I'll admit they succeeded in taking away a great deal of my self-esteem. Soon, I caught onto more and more of the little subliminal messages in their conversation. They got much entertainment out of paining me and literally tearing me apart.

Perhaps it was because I was a good student, or because I was a kind, unassuming person, but for whatever reason, I became the victim of the group. Because of this false sense of camaraderie, I allowed myself to believe that they really did want me as a friend. If only I had known that deep down they were just using me as a scapegoat to lash out all of their insecurities on, then maybe I could have saved myself a lot sooner.

Because it was virtually four against one, I felt helpless. I had no allies to back me up, so I continued to play the role of the victim. If I would've had one person to back me up, I would have felt stronger and more assertive. I knew that if I tried to fight back, I would just be further ridiculed. As the months of verbal abuse went on, I would come home from school each day in tears and cry to my mother about how horribly I was being treated. Both of my parents assured me that the girls were just jealous of me, and that they had to make fun of me to make themselves feel better. My parents always told me to remember that I was a better person, and that one day I would find real friends. To me, that day seemed like it would never come.

The Emotional Pain Was Not Worth It

As the year progressed, I began to dread going to school. I knew that they were making a mockery out of me and the emotional pain was more than I could bear. No matter what I did, my friends would find a way to turn it against me and use it as fuel for their own personal jokes. It got to the point where I even quit baton twirling. Baton was something that I genuinely liked, but my insecurities forced me to quit. I knew that their eyes were on me at all times, just waiting for me to make a mistake so they could use it against me the next day. Back then I didn't realize it, but they were just trying to put me down so that they could feel more powerful. I was too timid to confront them.

Eventually, all of the months of my agony and crying to my parents boiled up to a climax. I was just checking my mail on the Internet one day, and I came across a letter from one of my male friends that said, "I found this e-mail going around, and I thought you ought to see it." To my dismay, this e-mail was entirely devoted to destroying my reputation and making me look like a complete loser. The e-mail was harsh, cruel, humiliating, insulting, and degrading. It was during this moment that I had an epiphany.

I knew that I had let the abuse go on long enough, and I was not going to take it anymore. Although I cried hysterically upon reading the e-mail, I decided to show it to my mother, who was utterly horrified by its contents. My mom was enraged that anyone would stoop low enough to degrade someone behind their back just for sheer enjoyment, so she retaliated by e-mailing the author of the vicious e-mail back a little letter of her own that sought to put the girl in her place.

I was so happy that I was getting my justice because one of my friends had finally been caught in the act and was about to be punished. I don't know if I ever thanked the boy who showed me the e-mail enough. Whether he knew it or not, his courage and sense of justice changed my life that year. Thanks to this boy, my friends finally got what they deserved. Now, they had my mom against them and they no longer had me as a friend.

Real Strength and Pride

By the end of that school year, I learned a lot about myself and just how strong I really was without them. I was extremely proud of myself for standing up to my ex-friends. I proved that my internal strength was more potent than any of their harmful words. Although I successfully escaped from the friendship nightmare and found replacement friends, I still felt the emotional repercussions.

For the rest of elementary school, I felt insecure about my new friends because I was afraid that they would betray me and stab me in the back like my former friends did. It was hard for me to trust even my closest friends, because

I had been wounded so severely by my last painful experience, but eventually the tides turned.

Now, as a junior in high school, I have moved on and found a close group of friends that has made my life seem more complete. I feel as though I have gotten my justice, because now I am the one with genuine, loyal, trustworthy friends who I can rely on for anything, while my former friends drifted apart and became sort of lost.

In a funny way, my harsh experience has liberated me. It gave me character and enough courage to stand up for what I believe in. I will never allow myself to become a victim as long as I live.

I have learned that sometimes negative experiences can have positive outcomes. They provide us with the courage to go on through adversity and equip us with strength and perseverance.

In a way I am thankful that I was faced with such a negative situation because the same girls who sought to destroy my spirit actually succeeded in making me the empowered person that I am today. Although I will always harbor memories of that painful time in my heart, I can walk taller each day knowing that I am stronger because of it. *No one* can ever take that away from me.

Does Fitting In Really Matter?

Tamra Dawn

In the following selection, Tamra Dawn looks back on her school days, realizing that her unpopularity was no fault of her own. In fifth grade she started at a new school and experienced rejection and teasing by the more popular students. But as the years went on, it became clear that she had little in common with the popular cliques, and she found peace with herself when she finally found the right group of friends.

When I was already a mom with kids of my own, I re-met Anne, a girl who had been in my fifth grade class and every class after that, but who had been so quiet that I barely knew she existed. She came over for dinner one night with her kids. My husband asked her how she had liked the kids at the schools we had gone to together.

Her answer was simple—but to me it was stunning.

"I didn't have anything in common with them," she said.

Here we were, two girls in the same school who both felt out of it. But I had blamed myself. I thought [I] must not look right, act right, *be* right because I wasn't popular.

But Anne was equally outside of things and she didn't think it was her fault.

It was one of those Ally McBeal moments when things fall into place and you learn something important about yourself. What Anne said had also been true for me. I didn't have much in common with the kids in my new school. (I had moved there the summer before fifth grade.) I still played with dolls and they wanted to be grown up. I wanted to roller skate with boys and they wanted to kiss them. Later, in junior high and high school, I cared more about ideas and they cared more about looks and clothes.

But instead of seeing things for what they were as Anne did, I blamed myself, and my self-esteem suffered.

And I'll tell you a secret: If you think there's something wrong with you, no one will argue with you. They will agree with gusto.

It's a subtle thing—what you feel inside about yourself kind of gets projected out into the world, almost like invisible vibes that other people feel.

A Difficult Move

The summer between fourth and fifth grade, social disaster struck. My parents bought a house across town. I made my mom take me to the principals' office at school to tell them that I wanted to keep going to my old school—but they told us it was impossible.

After we moved, I had a great summer. I could have killed my father for waylaying the girl he saw walking past our yard into the house next door and telling her to come meet his daughter who was her age. But that awkward moment (I had just washed my hair and had it wrapped in a towel and didn't want anyone to see me looking like that!) bloomed into a friendship, and Claudia and I played together every day that summer and were friends for years to come.

When we played handball against my garage door or roller-skated around the block, we were joined by Ricky, this really cute boy who lived around the corner. He skated with us and chased us and told us dirty jokes that made us feel really grown up. Once, he skated up behind me and pulled down my zipper. I zipped it back up real fast and pretended to be mad but I really wasn't. In fact, I liked it. He paid attention to me, he clearly liked me and we had a great time together.

Off to a good start, right?

Rejected by Friends

All that changed once school started. I was so happy to find out that Ricky was in my class. But now that we were around other kids, he acted completely differently towards me. Suddenly, he wasn't my friend anymore. I don't know, maybe it was considered uncool in that class to be friends with a girl.

When he wasn't ignoring me, he was making fun of me. Here I thought I was going into this class full of strangers with at least one friend—and he had suddenly and without warning turned into an enemy.

And the kids at my new school were so different than the kids at my old school. The new kids didn't seem to play much, except ball games at recess. They—or at least the girls—were less concerned with games than with how their hair looked and with wearing the clothes that were the most in. They tried to be as grown up as possible, carrying purses and rolling their socks (we had to wear socks) down so low it looked like they weren't wearing any. And they weren't very nice and they weren't very friendly. Not a great place to be new.

There were the popular girls—the ones who were both pretty *and* smart and who wore just the right clothes. Then there were other girls who were already paired up with best friends.

This continued throughout junior high and high school. I always had two or three friends but they were chosen because I needed to be with someone, and not because I adored them.

That's how things went for years. I felt bad about myself but never, ever breathed a word if it to anyone.

A Lucky Break

Then, on the first day of 11th grade, I noticed Anne in my last period class. She was all excited about this group of kids she had gotten involved with over the summer. She had become involved in a project where high school kids who were doing okay in school were tutoring elementary school kids in a poor part of town. The tutors had been trained together and had formed a kind of group. Every day, she would tell me more about it.

That Saturday night, they were all going to the movies together, and Anne asked if I wanted to come.

Well, to make a long story short, I really hit it off with this crowd. They became my friends. I finally found the right fit.

And I finally realized that I was an OK person.

Better late than never.

Organizations to Contact

The editors have compiled the following list of organizations concerned with the issues debated in this book. The descriptions are derived from materials provided by the organizations. All have publications or information available for interested readers. The list was compiled on the date of publication of the present volume; the information provided here may change. Be aware that many organizations take several weeks or longer to respond to inquiries, so allow as much time as possible.

Chicks & Cliques

20432 Scioto Terrace, Ashburn, VA   20147
(703) 728-1712 • fax: (703) 729-7175
e-mail: amy@chicksandcliques.org
Web site: www.amydunne.com/chicksandcliques

This program designed by counselor and consultant Amy Dunne, is structured to work with girls faced with gossip, power struggles, and the like. Using group counseling, Dunne helps young women deal with these common problems. Her program won the 2006 Promising Practices Award from Character Education Partnership in Washington, D.C.

Girls Leadership Institute

(410) 878-2258
e-mail: simone.marean@gmail.com
Web site: www.girlsleadershipinstitute.org

The Girls Leadership Institute, founded by Rachel Simmons (author of *Odd Girl Out*), offers camps to develop conflict management skills and emotional intelligence for girls from seventh to twelfth grade. It is geared toward assisting them in their relationships and handling group dynamics, especially in school.

KidsHealth
e-mail: comments@KidsHealth.org
Web site: www.kidshealth.org

KidsHealth is the largest Web site for doctor-approved health facts for children and young adults. It was created by the Nemours Foundation's Center for Children's Health Media. A search for cliques leads to information on groups and how to cope with feeling left out.

Psych Central
55 Pleasant Street, Newburgport, MA   01950
(978) 922-0008
e-mail: talkback@psychcentral.com
Web site: www.psychcentral.com

The Internet's largest and oldest independent social network, Psych Central was created by mental health professionals and provides information on various mental health and relationship issues. There is information about cliques available on the site.

Teaching Tolerance: A Project of the Southern Poverty Law Center
400 Washington Ave., Montgomery, AL   36104
(334) 956-8200
Web site: www.tolerance.org

Teaching Tolerance was established in 1991 in part as an effort to improve interpersonal relationships and support equitable school experiences for American children. The Web site's Teens page includes personal stories, resources, and information about applying for a grant and how to win the opportunity to publish your personal experiences in the organization's newsletter. There are downloadable materials for young adults and parents/guardians, as well as a free e-newsletter. *Teaching Tolerance* magazine is published in September and January of each year. More than ten thousand schools participate in this organization's annual Mix It Up at Lunch Day program, designed to encourage students to sit with people who aren't in their group of friends in an effort to break down clique barriers.

For Further Research

Books

Patricia A. Adler and Peter Adler, *Peer Power: Preadolescent Culture and Identity*. New Brunswick, NJ: Rutgers University Press, 1998.

Erika V. Shearin Karres, *Mean Chicks, Cliques, and Dirty Tricks*. Avon, MA: Adams Media, 2004.

Heather Moehn, *Everything You Need to Know About Cliques*. New York: Rosen, 2000.

Sara Shandler, *Ophelia Speaks*. New York: Harper Perennial, 2000.

Rachel Simmons, *Odd Girl Out: The Hidden Culture of Aggression in Girls*. New York: Harcourt, 2002.

Susan Sprague, *Coping with Cliques: A Workbook to Help Girls Deal with Gossip, Put-Downs, Bullying, and Other Mean Behavior*. Oakland, CA: Instant Help Books, 2008.

Rosalind Wiseman, *Queen Bees and Wannabes*. New York: Crown, 2002.

Periodicals

Emily Perlman Abedon, "Crush the Cliques," *CosmoGirl*, September 2000.

Jerry Adler, John McCormick, Karen Springen, Daniel Pedersen, Nadine Joseph, Ana Figueroa, and Beth Dickey, "The Truth About High School: Cliques Fill Teens' Emotional Vacuum," *Newsweek*, May 10, 1999.

Liza N. Burby, "Clique Power," *New York Newsday*, August 28, 1999.

Dierdre Dolan, "How to Be Popular," *New York Times Magazine*, April 8, 2001.

Suzanne Kantra, "Click Cliques: Social Aspects of Playing Games On-Line," *Popular Science*, December 2000.

Susannah Meadows, "Meet the Gamma Girls," *Newsweek*, June 3, 2002.

Mike O'Brien, "Ten Tips for Dealing with Cliques," *Fort Worth Star-Telegram*, September 28, 2006.

Mark Rowh, "The In Crowd: The Not-So-Shocking Truth About Cliques," *Current Health 2*, October 2007.

Time "A Curse of Cliques," May 3, 1999.

Ann Trememan, "Sugar, Spice, and All Things Nasty," *The Times* (London), August 6, 2002.

Nancy Wride, "Cliques Are Part of Being a Teenager," *Los Angeles Times*, May 19, 1999.

Internet Sources

"Cool Kids and Losers: The Psychology of High School Students in Peer Groups and Cliques," http://sitemaker.umich.edu/356.tran/true_clique.

Elie Klein, "A Guy on Cliques," Whole Family.com, December 11, 2006, http://www.wholefamily.com.

"The Myth of High School Cliques," PhilsBlogging.com, June 1, 2008, http://philsblogging.com.

Daniel Terdiman, "Web Cliques Too Cool for School," *Wired.com*, July 25, 2003, http://www.wired.com.

"Transcript of Interview with Dr. Katie Gentile," In the Mix-Cliques Online, http://www.pbs.org.

Index

A

Abandoning friends and clique members, 68–69, 80–83

Academics vs. popularity, 114–118

Acceptance, 14, 20, 53, 70, 89, 119

Accountability for teenagers, 46–47

Adler, Patricia and Peter, 12

Adolescent behavior

  eighteen years of age, 31–32, 62–66

  fifteen years of age, 26–28, 81, 106–110

  fourteen years of age, 23–24, 41, 56

  grade-based associations, 24

  seventeen years of age, 29–30, 119–123

  sixteen years of age, 28, 90, 111–113

  thirteen years of age, 21–22

  twelve years of age, 20

  See also High school; Middle school

African students, 107

Alcohol, 31, 49, 83, 86, 87

American Teen documentary (Burstein), 14

Anger, 60, 76, 117–118

Anorexia nervosa, 36

Artist clique, 41

Athletics, 22, 28, 42, 90, 91, 93, 120

B

Banker (position in clique), 34–35

Belonging, 20–32, 71–73

Bengali students, 107

Best friends, 18, 35, 48, 50, 63, 68–69, 81–82, 126

Betrayal, 26, 69, 80–83

Blanco, Jodee, 97–105

Body and weight, 35–36, 54, 60, 63, 65

Bozo/rejects clique, 42–43

Bratz dolls, 36

The Breakfast Club (movie), 12–13

Breast implants, 35

Bullying

  being different and, 53–55

  in elementary school, 53–55

  by girls, 17–19

  labels and slurs, 56–61

  See also David and Goliath comparison

Bus (school) behavior, 23–26, 98

C

Caplan, Chelsea, 17–19

Cattiness of adolescent girls, 18, 19

Chang, Demi, 67–70

Chinese students, 108

Christmas holiday, 99–100

Clique novels (Harrison), 14

Clique positions, 34–35

Clothing. *See* Fashion (clothing)

Clueless (movie), 13

Coexistence of cliques, 38–43